*Wherever they may have come from,
and wherever they may have gone,
unicorns live inside the true believer's
heart. Which means as long as we
can dream, there will be unicorns.*

Bruce Coville in
INTO THE LAND OF UNICORNS

UNICORN
magic

Tess Whitehurst (Boulder, CO) teaches magical and intuitive arts in live workshops and via her online community and learning hub, the Good Vibe Tribe Online School of Magical Arts. An award-winning author, she's written eight books, which have been translated into eighteen languages. She has appeared on the Bravo TV show *Flipping Out* as well as morning shows on both Fox and NBC, and her writing has been featured in *Writer's Digest, Spirit and Destiny* (in the UK), and online at elephantjournal.com.

UNICORN
magic

Awaken to Mystical Energy & Embrace Your Personal Power

Tess Whitehurst

LLEWELLYN PUBLICATIONS
Woodbury, Minnesota

FIRST EDITION
First Printing, 2019

Book design and edit by Rebecca Zins
Cover design by Shannon McKuhen

Llewellyn Publications is a registered trademark
of Llewellyn Worldwide Ltd.

The Library of Congress Cataloging-in-Publication Data is pending.

ISBN 978-0-7387-6030-8

Llewellyn Publications
A Division of Llewellyn Worldwide Ltd.
2143 Wooddale Drive
Woodbury, MN 55125-2989
www.llewellyn.com

Printed in the United States of America

CONTENTS

Unicorns represent peace and harmony and a compassionate way of living. They teach us that those who possess true power, self-confidence, and wisdom tread gently in the world and care for the innocent and vulnerable . . . they give us hope. If we let them, they'll guide us toward a more enlightened existence.

Skye Alexander in
UNICORNS

INTRODUCTION

Only the pure of heart can see a unicorn.

Unicorns will only approach or befriend those with the noblest of intentions.

The unicorn's horn can transform even the most fetid swamp into a crystal-clear, pristine pond.

The unicorn's horn can also neutralize the most noxious poison.

A unicorn can perform miraculous healings by extracting and banishing the cause of any plague, illness, or infection.

As long as there is even one living human with the passionate desire to love and serve all of life, somewhere deep in the forest at least one unicorn runs wild and free.

Have you heard these legends? Even if you haven't, I'm guessing you can feel their symbolic truth in your heart. That's because some myths are not myths. Some myths are simply realities you haven't met yet ... although perhaps you *have* met the unicorn.

Perhaps you've met the unicorn when your eye caught sunlight dancing on water or when you inhaled the subtle scent of apple blossoms or bathed in the light of a full moon.

When raindrops trapped in a spider web sparkle, when a prism weaves sunlight into a tapestry of rainbows, and when the delicate tinkle of a wind chime is carried to you on the breeze, the unicorn is there.

Watching. Waiting. Beckoning.

Even now, the unicorn is inviting you to step into the magical realm that is your true home.

Whether or not you realize it yet, you are a powerful sorcerer or sorceress. You radiate power. You spread beauty and wonder wherever you go.

Perhaps you've forgotten this is your true identity or discounted your own intuitive memory of who you are, but the unicorn hasn't. The unicorn has been faithfully keeping this truth safe for you, waiting for the moment when you are willing to claim it, own it, and wield it.

As beings of immaculate integrity, unicorns hold a unique and precious space in our cultural consciousness. It is wonderful to see how popular they have become in recent years, as their values are so needed at this time: love and respect for all creatures and the interconnected web of life, the courage and initiative to do what is right, intense empathy and compassion, and a fierce resolution to protect and defend all that is pure at heart, including our beloved Mother Earth.

Clearly, it's not a coincidence that unicorns have become more visible in our culture at this time. They're a powerful medicine for all that currently challenges our world.

Like so many of us, I have felt a deep connection with unicorns since I was a child. In the years since then, I've felt compelled to study unicorn symbolism and to commune with unicorns in the inner realms as an aspect of my spiritual path. As you will see, they are unlike any other being in the way they combine fierceness and courage with gentleness and purity.

For many years, I have taught the magical and spiritual arts through workshops, books, blog posts, videos, and my online community, the Good Vibe Tribe Online School of Magical Arts. Across the board, the principles, practices, and values I teach—including love, wonder, purification, and magical empowerment—are perfectly aligned with the gifts of the unicorn.

Writing this book was an illuminating experience, as each facet of unicorn magic presented itself as a divine stream of energetic wisdom flowing through my awareness and onto the page. While I had studied unicorn lore somewhat thoroughly before I decided to write a book on the subject, I was surprised to feel wisdom's potent purity shine through as an alive channel of consciousness all its own. I was also surprised to discover the presence of unicorns not just in the West but also in the East, including India, China, and Japan. Clearly, the unicorn is a force to be reckoned with—not only across the globe and centuries but also within our individual and collective consciousness.

Each chapter of this book introduces a unique aspect of the unicorn's power and magic. You'll find inspiring pearls of unicorn wisdom as well as meditations, rituals, and exercises to attune you to the unicorn's realm and introduce you to practical ways you can work with unicorn energy to create positive change in your life and the world.

Once you've been thoroughly attuned, the final chapter offers a number of fun and empowering unicorn spells you can perform for specific purposes.

If you're irresistibly drawn to the beauty and mystery of unicorns, please don't discount this feeling as frivolous or fluffy. It's the unicorns calling you to a profound and powerful spiritual path. It's the unicorns asking you to participate in a powerful shift of consciousness that will allow much-needed multidimensional healing to occur on our planet. And it's the unicorns recognizing you as one of their own.

Have you ever wondered why you have always been so irresistibly drawn to the world of unicorns? Now you have an inkling. Would you like to know even more?

Are you ready to enter the portal?

Are you ready to live your magic?

Are you ready to be who you really are?

Knowing that the world
would cease to exist if the magic
died, the fairies chose the most exquisite
and enchanting creature in the universe
and sent it to earth, so that all who
looked upon it would fall under its spell.

Skye Alexander in
UNICORNS

one

WONDER

Exactly what is this world in which we find ourselves? Why do we seem to wake up each morning to this same human life in this same little corner of the universe we call planet Earth? What is going on here? And what could possibly be the point?

If you've been honest with yourself, you've certainly noticed that no one has any viable answers to these questions.

Still, I think you'll agree that if there is a point, it's almost certainly not to impress people with how cool we are or how many degrees we have or how many planes we've jumped out of or how many reality shows we've been on or how nice a house we live in or even how regularly we meditate.

Furthermore, it's safe to say your purpose here is not to be a consumer of products, critic of other people's work, or statistic in someone's data collection program.

And despite the relentless nature of the mystery and its unpredictable ways of manifesting in our lives (from winning a tropical vacation to getting two flat tires in the middle of a suspension bridge), if you really think about it, neither boredom nor jadedness nor disinterest seem to be a rational response either.

Because as relentless and unpredictable as it may be, no matter how much it fluctuates between beautiful and terri-fying, soul crushing and life affirming, this world in which we find ourselves is poised among a vast, glittering sky full of stars, expanding infinitely in all directions. Time is filled with mysteries we cannot fathom. Eyes glitter with emotion. Moments arise and then disappear forever, as if they were actually nothing more than dreams. Sunlight refracts into a full spectrum of colors. Hearts ache with love and beauty and grief. Plants grow. Flowers bloom. Leaves fall. Wood decomposes into soil, nourishing the forest for decades and centuries to come, and the whole cycle repeats itself again and again and again.

So just what is a rational response to all this mysterious beauty and heartbreak, fire and ash, dying and being reborn?

Wonder, that's what: pure, unadulterated wonder.

Whither Wonder?

It's no secret that most of us aren't going around feeling wonderstruck all the time. Even if a favorite song sometimes brings tears to our eyes or the full moon on a clear night occasionally takes our breath away, for many of us, wonder often feels like the exception rather than the rule.

But considering the wondrous conditions that constantly surround us and characterize our existence, it's logical to ask ourselves: What's the deal? Why aren't we feeling wonderstruck more consistently? Where in the world went our wonder?

There is a high probability you're already good and convinced that (A) our culture is currently in a state of desperate insanity, and (B) our personal perspective is largely shaped by the culture in which we are raised. So in lieu of wasting ink on such things, suffice it to say we know that A and B both possess a generous measure of truth.

As such, let's be compassionate about our lack of wonder, knowing that it's a byproduct of being born and raised in a world gone mad.

Simply having arrived at this conclusion means all is not lost. Acknowledging the discrepancy empowers us to consciously cultivate wonder. In so doing, we can bring sanity back and respond to this wondrous world with the generous measure of wonderment of which it is worthy.

In addition to being a plain old rational response to life, bringing our wonder back will kindle a fire of joy within us. It will make us a beacon of beauty and truth. It will allow us to set in motion towering waves of love and inspiration, which will in turn bring countless and immeasurable benefits to the world.

After all, even in a civilization gone mad, creatives still create. Inventors still invent. Healers still heal. And in every discipline, medium, and modality, the resounding results expand in proportion to the amount of wonder that's alive in the heart of the person who is the catalyst. Without wonder, the results of one's efforts are reliably commonplace. On the other hand, consider anyone whose work you admire, and you will realize that wonder is what fans the flames of boldness and ingenuity, elevating even the most everyday endeavor to the level of genius.

With all of this in mind, it is imperative that we find and reclaim as much of our mistakenly mislaid wonder as we possibly can. But where is it waiting? Whither has it wandered?

It hides in plain sight. It abides in your own mysterious depths. It dwells in the silent unknown.

The Silent Unknown

There is sound, but there is much more silence. There are planets, but there is much more space. There is movement, but there is much more stillness. There is light and there is darkness, but there is much more vast, open, empty expansiveness from which light and darkness both arise and in which they both appear.

Even now, your body is emptier and more invisible than it is solid and tangible. The very atoms of our physical selves contain much more space than they do matter. And once they dissolve into earth and sky and sea, where do we go? No longer dwelling in this time/space dimension in this present form, in a real sense we dissolve back into the eternity from which we came—the wild, mysterious infinity that is our true identity and our true home.

The following exercise will unblock and activate your magical consciousness by powerfully connecting you with the silent unknown.

UNICORN PORTAL KEY #1:

Sky Gaze

As you have perhaps already sensed, this book is a swirling invitation to step into your power and enter the current of some of the most nourishing magic there is: to live deeply, to open your heart, and to awaken to the iridescent enchantment of being alive. We'll call it entering the unicorn portal.

But entering the unicorn portal is not just a matter of reading words on a page. Rather, it's a shimmering, sparkling, multidimensional endeavor that requires you to proactively shift your consciousness and energy by taking concrete actions in the physical world.

In each chapter there will be a key. It may help to envision each one as an actual key you can hold in your hand, place on an oversized key ring, or wear on a ribbon around your neck.

This particular key is made of sparkling stars in a midnight-blue sky. When you hold the key and look at it from different angles in the light, it transforms from night to day, revealing a blue sky filled with sunlight, rainbows, and clouds before it transforms back again.

This key dearly wishes to be in your possession. But to obtain it, you must complete the following:

Sit outside in a relaxing place. It can be anywhere at all, as long as it's safe, relatively secluded from other humans, and you can see the sky. Turn off your phone or put it on airplane mode and set a timer for thirty minutes.

Now you will sky gaze. Place your attention on the firmament. Consider the beauty of the clouds, blue sky, or stars. Contemplate the vastness. Marvel at the mystery. Let your mind wander as it wishes through beauty, wonder, or simply rapt attention. When you notice your awareness has drifted to something other than the open space we call the sky (such as what you will eat when you get back or what you posted on social media earlier in the day), simply bring your attention back to the sky without chastising yourself in the slightest.

Be aware that boredom will likely creep in. If it does, smile at it. Continue sky gazing and begin to wonder if there is life on other planets. Also wonder what those planets and living beings might be like.

Once the timer dings (provided you have followed the directions as outlined above), you have earned the first key. Envision it. Examine it in your mind's eye. Look at it from all angles. Then imagine yourself sliding it onto a key ring or hanging it from a cord around your neck.

For practical purposes, be sure to also consider the following:

* Wear sunscreen, sky gaze at night, or
  stay in shade so you don't get burned.
* To protect your eyesight, don't
  look directly at the sun.
* You may want to bring a blanket, folding
  chair, yoga mat, pillow, or anything else that
  will make you more comfortable as you gaze.

Sparking the Fire

Unicorns are the guardians of wonder; they keep wonder alive. Conversely, the more wonder we feel, the more
unicorns thrive.

And even the most dazzling, shimmering, sparkling
infernos of wonder begin with a single spark.

That's why it's of utmost importance that we regularly
ask ourselves: Besides the obvious—the vastness of space
and the relentless mystery of the universe—what sparks
my sense of wonder? Of course, everyone's wonder sparks
are different, but here you'll find some simple items and
areas to consider.

I suggest that you find a beautiful journal or notebook,
as well as a beautiful pen. These can be wonder sparks in
themselves, so take the time to find ones that make joy
move upward in your belly like a sunlit fountain. Once

you've assembled your journaling tools, when a spark flies within you, write it down.

But first, write Wonder Sparks at the top of a page. Then make a list.

COLORS, TEXTURES, AND PATTERNS might spark your sense of wonder. Many of those with an affinity for unicorns love shimmery, sparkly things, as well as opal white, amethyst, aquamarine, teal, robin's-egg blue, rainbows, and the silvery color of the moon. But any and all colors may spark your sense of wonder: every visible color of the spectrum, as well as the invisible ones.

SOUNDS AND SONGS are reliable wonder sparks for many of us. Consider sounds that catapult you into the realm of the wondrous. Some perennial favorite sounds among those called by the unicorn include wind chimes, fairy bells, wind in trees, bird songs, the whirr of hummingbird wings, crickets, crackling fires, ocean waves, and mountain streams. Music is highly personal, but most of us have songs, artists, and genres we find ourselves coming back to again and again for their ability to remind us of the splendor and glory and mystery of life. What are yours?

NATURAL OBJECTS such as pinecones, acorns, feathers, crystals, and rocks, and **NATURAL SETTINGS** such as waterfalls, beaches, meadows, and caves can be wonder-igniters extraordinaire. Certainly you have your favorites; list the natural objects and settings that inspire you and fill you with awe.

PLANTS AND ANIMALS of all varieties—including, of course, the "mythical" variety—increase our sense of wonder and align us with the expansive and mystical world of nonhuman consciousness. Which ones never fail to do so for you?

SCENTS such as the pavement after it rains, your grandmother's favorite soap, blossoming lilacs, and freshly baked blueberry pie can be vibrant sensory portals into the great wide world of wonder.

LITERALLY ANYTHING ELSE that confers a sense of mystery, connection, and revelation also qualifies. This includes words, poems, articles of clothing, foods, beverages, cities, countries, languages, symbols, vehicles, holidays, planets, paintings, and seriously every other scintillating and awe-inspiring thing of which you can possibly conceive.

Fanning the Flames

To initiates of the unicorn path—those who seek not only to enter the portal but also to become an esteemed denizen of the realm—wonder is like oxygen, water, or sunlight: it is a necessity. To keep it in good supply requires many things of you, and while each of them is a responsibility, none is a burden. Rather, you will find all to be a boon.

First (as you will read more about in a future chapter), wonder cultivation requires you to be a devotee of beauty.

While the world-gone-mad would have us believe beauty to be a merely superficial concern, the true nature of beauty is anything but. It is an essential quality of the Wild Divine, also known as the Infinite, Source Energy, the Great Holy Mystery, and Who You Really Are. As such, seemingly everyday concerns such as tending to your garden, decorating your home, and brushing your hair are actually devotional acts, much like burning incense on an altar, pouring a libation of wine onto the soil, or blowing kisses to the sky.

Additionally, as a devotee of beauty, you must do your best to stop and inhale the scent of flowers as you encounter them, and to gaze at their petals as they quiver in the sunlight-dappled shade. You must remember to acknowledge the silvery crescent moon, wise old moon-beams, and the full moon's reflection in the puddles on the pavement. Similarly, devotees of beauty do not make coffee without inhaling the scent of the coffee beans first or make tea without considering the botanical ingredients and imagining the soil and sunlight in which they grew.

Sustaining wonder also requires you to cultivate mind-fulness and present-moment awareness.

In other words, rather than constantly planning for/worrying about the future or reminiscing about/rehashing the past, being in a state of wonder requires us to engage in what is often called *being here now*. This involves gently placing our attention on things like what is in front of us, who we are with, and how our body feels.

Of course, the human mind is in the business of wan-dering. Still, for wonder to infuse our consciousness as a matter of course, we must bring the mind back to the present moment repeatedly. Meditation teachers have been known to compare it to training a puppy that will never be trained or taming a monkey that will never be tamed.

Indeed, cultivating mindfulness is not about perfection: it's about patiently, lovingly bringing the mind back to the present moment again and again and again.

There are many practices to help you get into this habit. Meditation is one. If you've never meditated before, we live in a time when you can find countless free guided meditations via apps and online videos. Or, instead of meditation apps and recordings, you may prefer chanting mantras on beads, visualizing your body being filled with light, or setting a timer and repeating affirmations until it dings. Even five minutes a day makes a hugely positive difference. So you might start with five minutes and stay there or work your way up to as many minutes as you like.

Yoga is known to help with present-moment awareness. So is turning off your phone (or leaving it behind) and taking a solitary walk outside on a beautiful day.

Simply placing your attention on your breath is an invaluable mindfulness practice. When you notice your mind has wandered from the present moment, you can think, "Now I'm breathing in. Now I'm breathing out." In a more sustained way, you can practice keeping your attention on your breath when you are driving, walking, or even spending time with loved ones. You can feel the way it moves energy through your body and relaxes your muscles more and more with each breath. And when you notice your attention has wandered, you can simply, lovingly bring it back.

Additionally, those who would nurture wonder must be a familiar face to the natural world.

The sky beckons. The streams cajole. Even the soil pines for your luminous presence. Indeed, Mother Earth herself never fails to beseech. It is as if, in unison, they are reminding you (like any loving family would) to call more often, to stop by, to let them know when you'll be in town. In essence, they are saying, "We love you, child. Don't be a stranger. We like having you around."

You are a child of the earth and stars, and the earth and stars have not forgotten. You are a sibling to the waters, the plants, and the animals, and they know you as their kin.

Buildings are brilliant at keeping out the freezing cold and the blistering heat, as well as rain, snow, hail, mold, mosquitoes, and snakes. But don't let them keep you from your true home.

Even stepping outside for a few conscious minutes a day will keep you in the loop with the natural world. But things like hikes, picnics, walks, and even cups of tea on your patio will also help you and nature stay on companionable terms.

Without the natural world as your ally, family, and friend, your wonder will undoubtedly wither. So be sure to visit it often and marvel at its multifaceted majesty.

For full-on wonderstruck living, you must free up your imagination and believe wholeheartedly in the world of dreams.

Dreams are the pictures that appear to us as we sleep and the visions we conjure up in our imaginations. But what about what we call "real" life? Is it not dreamlike? Could it not possibly be a dream?

"Of course it isn't a dream," conventional wisdom teaches. "Real is real and dreams are dreams."

But it's a flimsy assumption.

Where does this thing we call "reality" appear to you? Exactly like dreams, visions, and fictional landscapes, it appears within your consciousness and nowhere else. How can you be sure, then, that one is real and the others are not? Because other people agree with you that "reality" is real? Those other people, though . . . where are they? They are in your mind only. Maybe they're somewhere else, too, of course, but it's impossible to be sure.

If a unicorn appears on your doorstep, then, is it more real or alive than if it appears in your dream or in your novel or in a mural you painted on a garden wall? As far as you know, each place is exclusively within your own consciousness, so you get to decide. What is real is completely up to you.

Of course, continue to perpetuate the mainstream illusion of an objective external "reality" if you want to. There's really no problem if that's what you want to do. It may be more comfortable for you, after all. But if you want to enter the unicorn portal, you're going to have to be quite a bit more logical. You're going to have to recognize that everything you can dream and everything you can imagine can also be real.

Speaking of imagining something into reality or dreaming something into being, those who would walk the path of the unicorn must believe in magic. Magic might be defined as your power to create positive change according to your will. Magic also includes things like the sacred power of trees and plants, the healing vibrations of crystals, and the mystical powers of herbs. (All of these will be covered at length in a future chapter.)

So, if you choose to read on, please be open to the realm of the mystical. And, even if you believe in magic already, be willing to expand your belief in what is possible. Remember the Shakespeare quote: "There are more things in heaven and earth, Horatio, than are dreamt of in your philosophy."[1]

---

1   William Shakespeare, *Hamlet: Prince of Denmark* (Princeton, NJ: John Bell, 1777), 24.

Living and Breathing
WONDER

To integrate all that you just read and to actualize it in your life experience, choose to perform at least three of the exercises below. For extra credit, do all six or do one of them more than once.

1   Make a wonder altar. Look back at your Wonder Sparks journal entry. Find a small surface and assemble items, colors, textures, etc., from your list as desired to create a shrine to the state of wonder. There are no rules other than that, but you might consider including classic altar items such as a cloth or scarf to cover the surface, an incense holder and incense, fresh flowers, and one or more candles in candle holders. A unicorn statue or image would also be a nice touch.

2   This assignment involves devoting a work of art to the quality of wonder. Use any medium you like. Compose or record a song, paint, write a poem, bake and decorate a cake, string prayer beads, plant a garden, write a blog post, sew some prayer flags, or make a short film. Or, truly, create art in any way that feels good

to you. Your Wonder Sparks journal entry may give you a hint of where to start or you could just let your intuition guide the way.

3   Turn off your phone or leave it at home. (Leave Instagram for another day.) Then take a leisurely walk through your neighborhood or a serene natural setting, paying close attention to the beauty as if you are in a three-dimensional, ever-changing museum or virtual reality world devoted to wonder...because you are!

4   Recline comfortably somewhere where you won't be disturbed. Breathe consciously and relax any tension in your body. Close your eyes and visit a breathtaking interdimensional dream realm. Chances are good you'll encounter a unicorn. Perhaps, for example, you will visit a sun-dappled meadow or a waterfall or a misty forest or a rainbow crystal cave. Walk through this world and pay attention to where you go, what you find, and who you meet. Be gentle, quiet, and loving, and listen deeply to the silent wisdom shared with you.

5   Make or purchase a small charm or piece of jewelry that speaks to your sense of wonder. For example, a unicorn pendant, a crystal, a charm bracelet, a painted rock, or a pure white feather might be just the thing. Once you've found this small yet powerful item, hold it in the light of the sun or the full moon to let it soak up the magical, purifying rays. Set the intention to let your talisman be both a reminder and an anchor of your decision and commitment to live a wonderstruck life.

6   Be a devotee of beauty in your personal environment. Open your eyes to how you can promote more exquisite loveliness in your space. Perhaps clearing clutter and creating a more ambient lighting scheme will serve you, or maybe it's time to bring in more crystals, shift the colors, or switch out old imagery with whimsical prints and paintings of the natural world.

*When the unicorn appears
within our life, it acts as a catalyst
for transformations we have either been
through or are about to go through.*

Ted Andrews in
TREASURES OF THE UNICORN

two

ALCHEMY

For many of us, the word *alchemy* brings to mind a bearded scholar in a hooded robe laboring away in an archaic laboratory, trying to discover the formula that will transmute base metals into gold. Historically speaking, this is not an inaccurate association with the word.

But such antiquated scenes were only an outer manifestation of an inner practice, one that appears in an unbroken, spiraling timeline extending both before and after the heyday of Shakespeare's Prospero. Indeed, since the earliest dawn of human spirituality, healing, and experimentation, there has been alchemy.

You might say that alchemy is the art and science of inner transformation, including the transformation of failure into wisdom, paralysis into power, pain into beauty, isolation into interconnection, limitation into freedom, and fear into love.

In turn, inner transformations like these have the potent ability to transform our outer world, first by affecting the way we interact with the external aspects of our lives, and consequently by shifting all of our life conditions, as well as—in substantial, if seemingly subtle, ways—the entire manifest world.

In other words, when our consciousness shifts, everything else also shifts. The unified field reverberates, affecting vast and significant changes in both visible and invisible realms. As such, in addition to being an empowering practice that will set you on the path of joyful self-mastery, alchemy is a vital key to the evolution of human consciousness and the healing of our world.

Now Hiring Alchemists

Have you ever laughed through tears and felt the heaviness in your heart dissipate, flowing upward like champagne bubbles sparkling in sunlight? Have you ever let music pulse through you until your body moved, your mind quieted, and you sensed your oneness with the moment (and possibly with everything)? Have you ever created literature or visual art about something that hurt you deeply and thus constructed universal beauty out of personal pain? If you've done even one of these things or something like it, you're already an experienced alchemist, and the whole world will benefit when you commit even more fully to practicing your art.

Of course, the fact that you are an alchemist should come as no surprise: those to whom the unicorn beckons are invariably alchemists. And those who answer the call—those who willingly pursue the elusive unicorn through the mystic inner realms, wherever it may lead—eventually feel compelled to become deliberate in their alchemical work. (Rest assured that reading this book means you are indeed answering the call.) So while you will still practice alchemy as a natural part of your everyday life—through practices such as laughing, dancing, and creating art—now you will be aware of what you are doing, and you will purposefully practice alchemy as an art form in its own right.

But what does it mean to practice alchemy deliberately? And how on earth does one begin?

Never fear, alchemist dear: answers are near.

Stardust Swirling

Everything is energy. You've probably heard that before, perhaps in science class or in one of a thousand other spiritual books. But have you ever thought about it? Have you felt it? Have you owned it? Have you tuned into the energy within you, which is also the energy within everything else, including the ocean, the sunlight, the air, the soil, and the swirling stardust? Have you gone beyond the words and into the truth they describe: that you can't possibly be anything other than infinity, and that you—the truth of you—is timeless, birthless, deathless, limitless, and omnipotent?

Conversely, it is equally miraculous and astounding that you are currently present in this earthly, seemingly finite form. There has never been anyone like you, and there never will be. The fact that you arose out of the mind-bogglingly vast number of potential genetic combinations present *in your parents alone* is entirely improbable and truly inconceivable. Indeed, from a macrocosmic standpoint, you are no less rare, precious, or extraordinary than a unicorn.

You are stardust briefly masquerading as a physical being. You are a precious creature animated with infinite wisdom, glowing and sparkling with the same energy that gave birth to the cosmos.

Now that you are considering your oneness with the oneness of all, consider that while all is indeed one, all is also two. Everything you see and experience is defined through the appearance of opposites: light and dark, movement and stillness, silence and sound. Without one polarity, the other would have no form, no outline. Without both light and dark, an image is not an image. Without both movement and stillness, a dance is not a dance. Without both silence and sound, a song is not a song. So while everything is one (in terms of energy), everything is also two (in terms of polarities), and the two give birth to all the countless things that you see and experience.

Awakening to the presence of both oneness and two-ness is one of the first lessons of alchemy. Doing so allows you to consciously establish greater balance between the polarities within yourself, your life conditions, and the world.

UNICORN PORTAL KEY #2:

Balance the Sun and the Moon Within You

Unicorns are aligned with both solar and lunar wisdom. Alchemically, the sun corresponds with what is called yang energy in Eastern alchemy and what is called masculine energy in the West. It is light, heat, day, expansion, action, structure, and the solid external world. The moon corresponds with yin, or feminine energy: dark, coolness, night, receptivity, stillness, fluidity, and the dreamy inner realms. An ideal balance of sun and moon qualities within you facilitates harmony, joy, vitality, abundance, peace, wisdom, self-mastery, general effectiveness, and greater ease in obtaining every form of success.

This key looks completely silver on one side, but when you flip it over, you discover the other half is pure gold. But the silver is not just silver: it also shines with an ethereal luminescence like the full moon on a clear night. And the gold side is not just gold: it also radiates a blinding golden-white brightness like the noonday sun. Again, this key is alive, and it actively desires to be in your possession. But first, you must complete the following:

Find a relaxing place where you will not be disturbed. This could be indoors or out, as long as it's completely private, comfortable, and safe. Sit or recline with your spine relatively straight and your arms and legs uncrossed. Close your eyes. Become conscious of your breath. Notice as you breathe in and notice as you breathe out. Notice how your breath naturally begins to deepen.

Bring your awareness to any areas of your body that feel uncomfortable or tense. Feel that you are sending breath to these areas as you breathe in, and feel that you are releasing tension and discomfort as you breathe out. Continue until you feel deeply relaxed.

Now, in the inner realm, visit a mystical lake at midnight. The sky is filled with bright stars and a huge, luminous moon that lights up the sky and is reflected on the mostly still but faintly rippling surface of the lake, dotted around the edges with white water lilies and lily pads.

A patch of blossoming lilacs to your left begins to stir, and in time a unicorn emerges, illuminated by the cool, vibrant moon. This creature's silvery coat and spiraling, iridescent horn shimmer in the moonlight. The unicorn approaches. You place your hand on the unicorn's mane and it gazes at you sideways, and you see that its eyes are the same sparkling midnight-blue color as the sky.

Although silent, you know the unicorn is lovingly communicating with you. Specifically, the unicorn is filling you with gentle lunar energy and wisdom. Although it does not deplete this magical being in any way, you feel the unicorn's light moving into your body. Somehow, you know this light is healing and balancing you perfectly because it has an innate intelligence all its own.

When the infusion is complete, you feel immense gratitude for this unicorn and realize that it is your own personal guide. Now it will share a name with you that you'll hear or see in your mind or that you'll just somehow know. Receive it with gratitude, knowing you can call on your unicorn's presence at any time for a balancing infusion of lunar energy and wisdom. (If you're not sure what your lunar guide's name is, ask yourself, "But what if I *did* know? What would it be?")

With great love in its sparkling eyes, your unicorn guide turns and softly trots back into the lilacs at the edge of the lake. Feeling deeply safe and loved, you fall asleep in the moonlight.

Soon you sense the bright sun directly overhead and open your eyes. From the position of the sun, you can see that you have slept not just through the night, but through the late morning as well. Now the lake sparkles like glitter in the sunlight. Notice that the water lilies are the purest possible white.

Gaze to your right and notice a shady grove of cedar trees. From deep inside the grove, a bright white unicorn emerges into the light. Its golden-white coat and spiraling gold and white horn blaze in the clear brightness of the day. This unicorn approaches, and you turn and place your hand on its mane. You see that its eyes are the same clear blue as the sky.

Although silent, you know this unicorn is powerfully communicating with you. Specifically, you are receiving a powerful infusion of strong solar energy and wisdom. Although it does not deplete the unicorn in any way, you feel light moving from the unicorn's body into yours. Somehow, you know this light is healing and balancing you perfectly because it has an innate intelligence all its own.

When the infusion is complete, you feel immense gratitude for this unicorn and realize that it is your own personal guide. At this time, your guide will share a name with you that you'll hear or see in your mind or just somehow know. Receive it with gratitude, and know that you can call on your guide's presence at any time for a vitalizing infusion of solar energy and power. (Again, if you're not sure what your solar guide's name is, ask yourself, "But what if I *did* know? What would it be?")

With powerful love in its clear eyes, your unicorn turns and energetically lopes back into the cedar grove, disappearing into the depths. Feeling energized and enlivened, you now come back from this inner journey.

Before you leave this relaxing space, take a moment to jot down your guides' names, as well as any insights you have into how to bring greater harmony and balance into your life. You will find you have a particular clarity on this topic after spending time with your lunar and solar unicorn guides. You may have insights into seemingly small things (like drinking more water, getting more sleep, or cleaning out your closet) or seemingly gigantic things (such as leaving a toxic relationship, moving to a new city, or changing your career path). Regardless of its perceived significance, write it down. Continue until you genuinely can't think of anything else. In other words, make sure not to leave anything out.

Once you've completed the above journey and journaling practice, congratulations: the key is yours. Gaze at it in your mind's eye and imagine yourself adding it to your astral key ring.

The Rainbow Connection

What if it *is* all unicorns and rainbows? What if everything else is an illusion?

I am not being facetious; I am asking in all seriousness.

As we saw in the last chapter, if you examine what you actually know to be "real," you will find there are no certainties. Everything, after all, is filtered to your awareness through your senses. So can we trust that what we perceive exists outside of our consciousness? Alas, we cannot. As such, we are living a life that is not much different than a dream.

In this dream we call life, everything that appears in our field of vision is shaped and defined by color and light.

We are told that our eyes actually evolved the way they did because of our sun and that the pure white light of the sun is refracted in a million different ways to form all that we see.

So, in an actual sense—at least visibly speaking—it *is* all rainbows.

Still, the question remains: Is it also unicorns?

The literal answer is no. You cannot look under a microscope and see that everything is made up of tiny unicorns. We are not generally observing light from the sun being bent or refracted to create the appearance of unicorns. In fact, if you look in the index of any science book, you are not likely to see unicorns listed even once.

On the other hand, unicorns are a symbol of all the most precious things about human consciousness: wonder, imagination, courage, purity, creativity, positivity, fairness, wisdom, joy, and the power to heal. Albert Einstein wrote, "Imagination is more important than knowledge. Knowledge is limited. Imagination encircles the world."[2]

Imagination encircles the world.

So, yes: symbolically speaking and from the perspective of human consciousness, in addition to being all rainbows, it is also all unicorns.

2   Walter Isaacson, *Einstein: His Life and Universe* (New York: Simon and Schuster, 2017), 387.

And they are closely related. Just as rainbows give birth to every visible thing, the imagination and wonder that are the unicorn's domain allow humans to refract and recombine the pure light of consciousness into our own spiritual and scientific evolution—all that we invent, conceptualize, and create.

To celebrate and integrate the astonishing truth that it is all rainbows and unicorns, I suggest that you take a break from reading and use your imagination to create something beautiful now. It could be a painting, a poem, a song, a flower arrangement, a cake, an equation, or something else entirely.

Solve et Coagula

Solve et coagula is a favorite adage of the alchemist. It means "dissolve and reform." You might say a rainbow dissolves the appearance of pure light and reforms it into color. In turn, this color forms every visible thing. Through creativity and imagination, the unicorn dissolves the appearance of the mundane world and reforms it into magic. Magic is your ability to create positive change in your life in accordance with your will and desire.

In case you harbor the least bit of doubt, let me assure you: you have that ability. You are an alchemist. You are magical. As sure as you can grind up coffee beans and transform them into a fresh and delicious cup of coffee, you can dissolve conditions you don't love and transform them into conditions you do.

If you don't believe me, close your eyes and ask your unicorns. (See? I told you.)

In your journal or on a piece of paper, make two vertical lists, side by side. In the first, write what you would like to dissolve, and in the second, across from what you'd like to dissolve, write what you'd like to reform. For example, the "dissolve" list could include health challenges, fear or anxiety, patterns of lack, a job you don't love, a toxic relationship, or any other thing you don't currently find to be ideal. Respectively, items in the "reform" list might include vibrant health, patterns of abundance, a career path you adore, confidence and calm, a healthy relationship, and so on.

The Phoenix and the Butterfly

Both the phoenix and the butterfly are friends of the unicorn: they are symbolically and mythically intertwined. Not coincidentally, both are also synonymous with extreme and miraculous transformation: both creatures dissolve and reform to the absolute utmost. Letting go of the old in a radical and even painful way, they then spread their vibrant, breathtaking wings and fly.

Now it's time for you to do the same.

First, choose a transformation totem: the phoenix or the butterfly. Which will it be for you at this time of your life? Here are some things to consider:

The phoenix sheds, burns into ashes, and rises up from those ashes fully formed and fiery. Perhaps a century later, this happens again. Another century later, it happens yet again. In fact, as the centuries go by, the phoenix finds herself in an endless cycle of living, dying, and being reborn. The phoenix's wisdom and power particularly speak to people who have been through so much trauma, pain, grief, or heartache that it has felt like they were dying. In fact, what they have been doing is burning through old karmic expectations and debts in order to become stronger, wiser, and more beautiful than they otherwise could have been.

The butterfly universally starts as a caterpillar. One day that caterpillar inexplicably feels like creating a cocoon around himself, retreating from the world. In time, he feels an irresistible desire to break out of the cocoon. The process of doing so entails more pain and struggle than he previously could have imagined. And then, at long last, he finds he has utterly transformed. He is a new creature, one of the most beloved in nature: he is a butterfly. Butterfly medicine appeals to people who are at a pivotal point in their development. After an extended period of struggle and hard-learned lessons, they feel ready to break free and transform into the most powerful and beautiful version of themselves. They may not have previously understood the full meaning of what they were going through, and they may still not, but they nevertheless feel the irresistible instinct to fully free themselves from their cocoons, subsequently extend their beautiful wings, and fly.

After reading the above descriptions, you may be thinking that you want to choose both. Actually, though, one of them is calling to you more than the other. Relax. Allow. Choose. Then, if you feel a sense of disappointment after you choose, choose the other one instead. When you've settled on the one that will be most powerful for you, you'll feel at peace with your choice. (But it's not set in stone; if you do this exercise during a different time in your life, you could feel more drawn to the other one.)

On the other hand, if you read the above descriptions and you're thinking, "I'm not transforming that much right now, so I don't feel drawn to either," I must respectfully disagree. Your selection of reading material proves otherwise. The unicorn does not beckon to those for whom radical transformation is not an ongoing and present-moment issue. But if you're honest with yourself, you already knew that. So breathe, relax, and go deep.

How are you transforming right now? What are you releasing, and what are you becoming? How are you ready to be remade, redefined, or reborn?

Once you've chosen, revisit your list from the above section. If it's in a journal or notebook, tear it out. If you'd like, you can add to it if you think of something else or amend it if something doesn't seem quite right to you.

IF YOU CHOSE THE PHOENIX, get yourself a big red pillar candle and place it in a large cauldron or pot in which it is safe to burn things. Also gather a lighter or matches, metal tongs or tweezers, a terra-cotta pot, some potting soil, and a potted bright red or orange flowering plant that will do well indoors or on your patio.

Light the candle. Tear or cut the dual list in half so the conditions you want to transform are separate from the conditions you want to create. Read the old conditions you want to transform aloud and then safely burn them with the candle, using the tongs or tweezers if necessary and letting the ashes fall into the pot. As they burn, say or think:

> *I release you. I dissolve you. I surrender*
> *you. I transform you. I burn you away*
> *into fire. I burn you away into dust.*

After the paper is as thoroughly burned into ashes as you can comfortably make it, blow out the candle. When all the paper's ashes and charred remains are well and truly extinguished, put some potting soil in the bottom of the pot, mix the ashes in with it, then plant the flower on top of it. Remove the candle from the cauldron, wash or rinse the cauldron, and wash your hands. Read the new conditions aloud to the flowering plant, mentally empowering and enlisting this vibrantly alive being with your beautiful new intentions. Whenever you water and care for the plant, feel that you are nourishing these new conditions and steadily bringing them alive.

Please note: not many potted flowers are easily sustainable indoors. With this in mind, don't worry if your potted flower comes to its natural end. This need not reflect on the effectiveness of your ritual. Simply release it to the earth or a compost bin and see it as another part of the phoenix's constant cycle of transformation.

IF YOU CHOSE THE BUTTERFLY, pull everything out of your clothes closet and put it on your bed. Also pull everything out of your dresser drawers. Clean the inside of the drawers and closet thoroughly. Gather a bundle of dried feather or desert sage (available online and at many health food stores and metaphysical supply shops), a small dish or plate, and a lighter or matches. Light the bundle so that it's smoking like incense, and hold the dish beneath it to catch any burning embers. Waft the smoke around yourself, the inside of your closet, and even inside and around your dresser. (This will release and transform old, stuck energy.) When this feels complete, extinguish the sage by sealing it in a jar or running it under water.

Next, read aloud the things you are releasing and transforming. After you read them, say:

> *I willingly surrender these old conditions. I release them*
> *completely in all ways and make room for the new.*

Next, put every piece of clothing back in your closet and dresser, but only if you love it and feel wonderful and energized when you look at it. If it doesn't empower you or excite you, or if it reminds you of any old condition that you're ready to release, put it in a pile on the floor. Once everything is either put away or piled on the floor, put the items in the pile in a box or bag and make plans to donate them to a charity of your choice.

Now, read aloud the conditions you are calling in and reforming. Once you've read them, say:

> *I welcome and give thanks for these beautiful new*
> *conditions in my life. I embrace the most beautiful*
> *and powerful possible version of myself now.*

Feel this to be true in your heart. With as much present-moment self-love and self-approval as you can muster, take another moment to consider making a radical or otherwise refreshing change to your appearance. For example: a new hairstyle, a tattoo, a piercing, or even a strength-training regimen would do the trick. (Although you can certainly choose more than one.) It's a good sign if the very idea feels both wildly exciting and slightly terrifying, like something you sincerely want to do but up until now have not admitted to yourself or considered but then dismissed. Perhaps you even said or thought something like, "It'd be fun to dye the ends of my hair pink (or have super strong muscles or a nose ring or whatever), but that just isn't me." But what if it *is* you? What if it's an aspect of you that previously has been hidden or denied? What if it's the *you* that you are becoming? (Spoiler alert: it is.)

Keep in mind that whatever change you choose, it's simply an outer symbol of a much deeper inner transformation. Also keep in mind that symbols can be very powerful indeed.

Once you've settled on a change, patiently make arrangements for it in the best and most loving way possible, doing so with great reverence and devotion toward your newly emerging butterfly self.

Unicorns purify us, for their purpose
is to trigger the innocence of the divine
self, that essence we had the moment
we became a divine spark. They
remind us of who we truly are.

Diana Cooper in
THE WONDER OF UNICORNS

Living and Breathing ALCHEMY

To integrate all that you just read and to actualize it in your life experience, choose to perform at least three of the exercises below. For extra credit, do all six or do one of them more than once.

1. Clear all the clutter from your home. As mundane as it may sound, nothing facilitates alchemical transformation quite as powerfully as decluttering. The fact that we must declutter at regular intervals throughout our lifetime reflects the fact that life is a process of constant change. Doing so with the intention to transmute unwanted old conditions into beautiful new ones adds potent fuel to the alchemical fire.

2. Get crystal talismans to represent your unicorn allies. Obtain a moonstone to help you attune to the frequency of your lunar unicorn ally. Obtain a sunstone to help you attune to your solar unicorn ally. Cleanse both in running water. Empower the moonstone in the light of the full moon, and empower the sunstone in the light of the noonday sun on a cloudless day. When

making contact with your allies during meditation (or anytime), hold the moonstone in your left hand (which is aligned with your receptive lunar energy) and the sunstone in your right hand (which is aligned with your active solar energy). You can also meditate with one in each hand to facilitate deep inner balance and equilibrium.

3 Hang a prismatic crystal in a sunny window. Because rainbows.

4 To further reinforce the positive changes you set in motion with the phoenix or butterfly ritual, find or make a piece of jewelry, a décor addition, or an altar item that depicts your transformational totem.

5 Laugh deeply, cry deeply, or both. Laughing deeply and crying deeply are both powerful alchemical practices that go deep into your body, mind, and emotions to transform stuck energy into inspiration and joy. It doesn't matter how you bring about those giggles or tears, just as long as they're authentic. For example, you might watch a sad or hilarious movie, have a heart-

to-heart with a parent about deep childhood pain you know you need to bring out into the open, or spend time with a friend or sibling who always makes you laugh.

6 Create beautiful art out of desperate pain. Particularly if you engaged in the phoenix exercise, you will find great power in creating new beauty out of old pain. Do not worry about making other people sad; often when we share our deepest sadness as a work of art, we actually help other people feel less alone and see a greater pattern and purpose in what they have endured.

The young unicorn
represents innocence and purity.
The unicorn's magical spirit brings
creation into the world of matter; it
symbolizes the Spiritual Gateway to
the higher realms of the Divine.

Cathy McClelland in
THE STAR TAROT

three

PURITY

Somehow, we all intrinsically and inexplicably know that unicorns relate to divine purity, which includes purity of mind, body, spirit, energy, intentions, and emotions. This is the power of the archetype. An archetype is like a waking dream symbol that is common to a large number of humans. If symbol and myth are the language of the psyche, an archetype is a word in that language—a word we instantly understand without ever having been taught. There's also some truth in describing an archetype as a universal interdimensional talisman: we see it, we dream about it, or we think about it, and some of its essence is conferred directly into our being. We paint it, we study it, or we meditate on it, and we conjure up its power to create positive change in our lives.

The Pure of Heart

What does it mean to be pure of heart? Is *your* heart pure?

As you may know, according to ancient Vedic wisdom, there is a chakra, or energy center, in the middle of your sternum called the heart chakra. This is your emotional center and the area of your body and energy field that corresponds with giving and receiving love. Even if you've never heard about this chakra, you know about it quite well: it's the area that hurts when you feel grief, flips when you swoon, and swells when you hold a puppy.

In Sanskrit it's called the *anahata* chakra, which may be translated into "unstruck." Some say this is the name for the heart chakra because in order for our hearts to be fully open, we must cultivate the emotional state that resembles that of a child who has never been deliberately punished or wounded in any way. In other words, our heart must be unguarded; as the popular slogan goes, we must love like we've never been hurt.

When the heart chakra is unguarded, we see into the true, lovable, and loving nature of every living thing and the entire universe: the interconnection of all that is and the singular unified field. Our wariness lifts and dissolves away, and we are able to glimpse what is really going on here, which—despite any appearances to the contrary—is actually nothing but love.

This is the true nature of your heart and Who You Really Are: love. Pure love. From that pure love stems pure courage, pure peace, and a pure knowing that you are one with the Infinite, as well as with all other beings on earth.

So is your heart pure? Ultimately and at its core, yes. Its true nature is purity. But are you currently experiencing it as pure? Maybe … or maybe not. Many of us go in and out of experiencing our hearts as pure. Such a tender feeling in this sometimes rather harsh human world requires us to consciously purify ourselves at the heart level. It also requires us to learn ways to shield ourselves in the truth of love so we are not endlessly drawn into the illusions of suspicion, competition, struggle, and lack. With both of these tasks, the unicorn's sparkling, spiraling horn can help.

The Sparkling Spiral

From a seashell to a hurricane to the whirling flutter of a falling leaf, nature spirals. Spirals are among the most primordial and universal human symbols, appearing in cave paintings, pyramids, and sacred texts all over the ancient human world. For kundalini yogis, life-force energy spirals upward from our tailbone and then throughout our body via the spinal column. In Greek mythology and modern medicine, the Rod of Asclepius, with its spiraling snake, is an eminent symbol of healing. And, of course, Watson and Crick famously discovered that DNA—the very building block of all life as we know it—possesses an intrinsic spiraling pattern.

Similarly, the unicorn's luminescent horn has been much coveted for its ability to send its spiraling magic throughout anything it touches. It's been said nothing can purify or heal quite as instantly, reliably, or completely.

The following exercise will purify you at the heart level, further attuning you to the frequency of the unicorn and further opening the portal to the realm.

UNICORN PORTAL KEY #3:

Detoxify the Heart

In the Middle Ages, alleged unicorn horns could fetch a shockingly high price for their fabled ability to neutralize all poisons. Similarly, unicorn sightings have often involved the unicorn touching their horn to a body of water and causing the water to bubble and swirl as a visible effect of the unicorn horn's purifying dynamic.

This exercise unlocks a purity key: when you have it, you will have greater access to the unicorn's magic because your heart will be pure. This key is a bright, iridescent white, and it spirals at its point like a miniature unicorn horn.

To begin, find somewhere quiet where you won't be disturbed. Sit with your spine straight in a comfortable way. Close your eyes. Place your attention on your breath. Notice as you breathe in and notice as you breathe out. Notice your breath naturally begin to deepen. Become aware of tension anywhere in your body. Send breath to it and allow it to naturally soften and relax.

Become aware of your stomach area. See or sense a radiant sphere of white light behind your bellybutton. As you breathe in, see or sense this light getting even brighter. As you breathe out, see it expanding to fill even more of your body. Continue breathing in (and seeing it get brighter) and breathing out (and seeing it get bigger) until this light completely fills and surrounds your entire body. See and sense every cell transforming into light. Feel light and energy flowing all the way down to your fingers and toes, and all the way up to the crown of your head.

Now become aware of your heart area: the emotional center that feels both love and grief. See or sense it as a still, serene alpine lake, filled with deep, cold water. If there is heaviness, armor, or any other stuck energy in your heart, you might get the sense that the water in this lake is not entirely clear or clean. Don't be alarmed by this.

Call now on your sun-aligned unicorn guide: the guide that emerged from the cedar grove during the previous chapter's meditation. When this unicorn arrives in front of you, request that it detoxify and activate your heart chakra. You will sense your unicorn nod or simply look at you lovingly in silent agreement. Your guide will then stoop a majestic glowing head down toward you and lovingly touch a golden-white horn to the alpine lake at your heart center.

Feel your heart area swirling and becoming purified. See it being filled with spiraling sparkles of blinding gold and white. Breathe deeply. Sense that all toxins, heaviness, and darkness are being neutralized and removed. Continue to breathe until this process feels complete. Your solar unicorn guide will then meet your eyes with even more love. See and sense the alpine lake at your heart chakra as completely clear and pure, reflecting the vibrant blue of the sky.

Thank your unicorn guide with the potent pool of energy at your heart center. Feel gratitude and love expand to encompass this solar guide, and feel it boomerang right back to you. Love is a magical thing that never depletes itself; love given freely always generates even more love.

The purity key is now in your possession. Admire its brightly shining iridescence and place it on your etheric key ring.

When you feel ready, open your eyes and come back to the place where you're sitting.

Creating Sacred Space

The pure of heart need a home that is not just shelter, but also sacred space: a consecrated temple, a magical laboratory, and a vortex of spiritual power. And where you live now can be that sacred space. It doesn't matter if it's big or small, grand or humble, rural or urban. It also doesn't matter if you live alone or with others, or whether you own, lease, or camp out in someone's basement.

Actually, where you are now is already sacred, if for no other reasons than two: (A) it's built on our sacred

Mother Earth, and (B) it's inhabited by such a sacred being as you. (Remember: in truth, you are a divine, eternal being. As such, the very earth you walk on is sacred. Not just because our planet is sacred all on its own, but also because you walk on it.) The idea, then, is to recognize and treat it as sacred. That way, your pure, loving, magical heart will have a place to blossom and thrive.

Begin by choosing to love where you live, wherever it is and whatever it looks like. Be aware that choosing to love where you live does not mean you have to live there forever. It simply means that you appreciate it and reverently treat it as a home for your spirit in this singular moment in time. (There is only one moment, after all.)

If you don't already love where you live, you can start by loving that you have a place to live at all—somewhere that keeps you safe, warm, and dry. You can further love that the land on which your home was built remembers its free and wild nature. Once you acknowledge and honor this truth, you will find that the ground beneath your feet emanates a sacred healing vibration all its own.

Once you've made the simple inner shift into loving and appreciating where you live, the following practices will further guide you along the path to establishing sacred space: space that protects your pure heart (thereby keeping you aligned with the unicorn realm) while promoting energy, vitality, peace, serenity, inspiration, creativity, harmony, clarity, and love.

CLEAR YOUR CLUTTER

As much as possible, free yourself of the burden of stuff. In the wise words of author and tidying expert Marie Kondo, "I can think of no greater happiness in life than to be surrounded only by the things I love. How about you? All you need to do is to get rid of anything that doesn't touch your heart. There is no simpler way to contentment."[3]

CLEAN

The forest, the unicorn's natural domain, has its own self-cleaning mechanisms: namely, the elements. The earth receives decay and transforms it into rich soil that feeds the fragrant flowers and trees, which in turn clean toxins out of the air. The air blows dead leaves from the trees and clears the earth of brittle vegetation. The sunlight powerfully purifies and disinfects. Rain falls and makes everything sparkle, burgeon, and bloom with fresh vitality. That's why spending time in the forest makes us feel so clean.

---

3   Marie Kondo, *The Life-Changing Magic of Tidying Up: The Japanese Art of Decluttering and Organizing* (Berkeley, CA: Ten Speed Press, 2014), 202.

Indoor spaces, on the other hand, need us to embody the elements on their behalf. The good news is that cleaning to create sacred space is much more satisfying than plain old cleaning to clean, and the only difference is the intention behind it. When wiping down surfaces and washing windows, set the intention to embody a rainstorm. When vacuuming or sweeping, be the wind. And, of course, you can also honor nature and the elements by selecting earth-friendly cleaning products and ones that are scented with natural essential oils.

CLEAR AND BLESS THE ENERGY

Meadows and woods aren't just physically clean: they're energetically clean as well. Being open to the sky and elements and filled with forest fauna and flora confers an invisible yet palpable aliveness and ambience.

Of course, your interior living space can't be the forest, but you can fine-tune it in such a way that brings in some small measure of that vastly sacred ambience.

In legends of both Western and Eastern origin, the presence of a unicorn is often accompanied by the sound of tinkling bells. So to begin to clear the space in your home, obtain or locate a bell, a string of bells, a chime, or a wind chime that has a fresh, clean, brightly tinkling sound. Ring or jingle it repeatedly as you move in a counterclockwise direction throughout each room and area of your home. As you do so, feel, imagine, and sense that the sound's vibrations are moving into every corner and molecule of the space, raising and purifying the energy as you go.

Unicorns are also said to have an affinity for the scent of cinnamon. Aromatherapeutically, it purifies the space and attunes it to the frequency of spiritual sweetness. So next, light a stick or cone of cinnamon incense. While carrying a dish or plate beneath it to catch any burning embers, again move in a generally counterclockwise direction throughout each area and room. (Metaphysically, counterclockwise is the direction employed for cleansing, clearing, unwinding, and unbinding.) When this is complete, you can place the incense in an incense holder and allow it to burn all the way down, or if that's quite enough smoke for you already, you can extinguish it.

Lilacs are another botanical associated with unicorns. If you magically happen to be close to a blossoming lilac tree, gently and lovingly snip a bloom. Pour spring water in a clear glass bowl and use the flower to asperge (fling water drops) lightly around your space. Move in a clockwise direction this time to seal in the positive energy.

If you don't happen to be near a blossoming lilac tree (which is likely: they only bloom for a short time and in specific climates), the next best thing would be to obtain some actual lilac essential oil and add ten to twelve drops to a mister of spring water. (I say "actual" because lilac essential oil is also somewhat elusive: it's not generally a mainstay at holistic health centers and health food stores. That's why, if necessary, you can substitute jasmine absolute or essential oil of ylang-ylang. Just be sure that whatever you use is 100 percent natural.) While moving in a clockwise direction throughout each room and area, shake the mister and lightly mist the space to set the sacred vibration in place.

To keep your space feeling sparkly and sacred as can be, you can repeat this process, or any part of it, as you feel guided. The more you align with the realm of the unicorn through reading and performing the exercises in this book, the more you will be unlocking your sensitivity. When your space needs fine-tuning, you'll be able to sense it. Trust what you sense.

VIBE UP YOUR DÉCOR

It's possible that your décor is already good and vibed up, or it may need a little tweaking, a partial makeover, or even a complete overhaul. It doesn't need to be fancy or expensive. In some cases, vibing up your décor could involve releasing things rather than bringing in anything new. Just ask yourself these key questions:

Do you love all your artwork, and does it depict something you'd like to experience? Imagery is powerful. If a picture, painting, or sculpture in your home depicts an energy, mood, or condition that you wouldn't want to call into your psyche and life experience, get rid of it. And if it doesn't uplift you and bring you joy, get rid of it. Then, if it's time for some new artwork, choose pieces that make your heart sing.

If you have plants, are they all vibrantly healthy? To establish space in your home that is sacred in the way a forest is sacred, your potted plants must be lush, nourished, and green. If any of your plants aren't healthy, do your best to nurse them back to health. If you see no improvement in a couple of weeks or so, give them to a friend with a green thumb or release them back to a compost heap or the earth. (Trust me: it's best for everyone, including the plant.)

If you don't have plants, would you like some? After all, the forest is filled with trees. The energy in your own personal sacred space will benefit immensely from a healthy parlor palm, a peace lily, or some lucky bamboo. (Or really any other kind of plant that you would feel good having around.)

Is your home comfortable and uplifting? Do you feel magical, relaxed, and inspired when you're home? Does spending time at home rejuvenate you? If not, what could you change in order to answer yes to these questions? For example, maybe your couch could use a soft, purple throw blanket, maybe a less-than-inspiring view from one of your windows could use a sheer and colorful curtain, or maybe the sound of running water from a desk fountain will help your home become the sanctuary you crave.

Set up an altar. If you haven't already, anchor the sacredness of your space with an illuminated hub of divine inspiration, also known as an altar. An altar may be small or large, elaborate or simple, hidden or in plain view. You may set it up on a shelf, a tabletop, or a corner of a countertop or workspace. If you live in a small or shared space, you could even set it up inside a closet. (If possible, though, it's a great idea to place it in such a way that you can sit in front of it for your visualizations and other meditative exercises in this book.) The important thing is that gazing at it uplifts you, energizes you, and encourages your sense of wonder.

For the purposes of this book, it's best if the central item, or focal point, of your altar is a depiction of a unicorn. This could be a small framed postcard or gift card, a larger framed painting or drawing, a statue, or even a glass or porcelain figurine. If you'd like, you could also find or create two depictions: one to represent each of your unicorn guides. Take your time to find or make something you love.

Add at least one candle in any color (or all colors!) of the rainbow, and your image will become an altar. You can stop there or add other items as well, such as incense in an incense holder, flowers, apples (unicorns love them), crystals, or anything else that feels right. You might also consider adding an image of the phoenix or the butterfly (whichever one you chose in the last chapter). Some people like to spread an altar cloth underneath it all before they position everything, but this is not necessary. Just make sure you love everything you choose and that it feels right when you place it on the altar. Tweak it until it clicks.

Do be aware that altars need tending. They're not mere décor: they are living, breathing portals between the everyday realm and the realm of magic. This means you don't want your altar to just sit there and collect dust. For example, regularly light the candle, cleanse the crystals in running water and sunlight, and keep the flowers fresh. Also rearrange it as often as the mood takes you. If you sit in front of the altar when you meditate and perform other exercises from this book, those would be ideal times to tend to these concerns.

Mind (as well as metals and elements) may be transmuted, from state to state; degree to degree; condition to condition; pole to pole; vibration to vibration.

The Kybalion

Raising Your Vibrations

At the quantum level, everything vibrates. And, as the law of attraction states (in the phrasing of Abraham-Hicks), that which is like unto itself is drawn. So when you raise your vibration, you improve what you attract into your life experience. If you vibrate at the frequency of harmony, you attract harmonious conditions. If you vibrate at the frequency of heart purity, you attract those who are pure at heart. If you vibrate at the frequency of joy, you attract more to be joyful for.

Acknowledging this dynamic also makes it clear when we are vibrating at a frequency that is not serving us, and it asks us to take responsibility for what we attract. For example, when we repeatedly seem to experience toxic relationships, we must ask ourselves: Where in my vibration am I holding the energy of relationship toxicity? Is it an expectation or pattern I've learned from my past? Is it a behavior of my own that can be described as toxic? Is it a deeply buried (but very present) belief that I don't deserve healthy relationships?

Taking responsibility doesn't mean blaming yourself or beating yourself up. We are all in the school and playground of life. As divine beings, we have chosen to be temporarily incarnated into this human experience in order to practice and play with vibration. You might liken it to a child choosing to learn gymnastics or ballet: should she berate herself when she falls off the balance beam or wobbles on her toe shoes? Should she wonder what is wrong with her and why she wasn't born ready for the Olympics or the Royal Ballet? Of course not! It's all part of the process. What would be the point in practicing if she already did everything perfectly? No destination means no journey, and no journey means no fun.

In addition to simply being aware of the dynamic of vibration and attraction, the following practices will allow you to reach greater and more consistent levels of heart purity through raising your vibration, which will in turn improve the quality of all that you attract. (Although every practice in the book will have a vibration-raising effect.)

Do keep in mind that while on the infinite divine level everyone is perfect, on the finite human level no one is perfect. So expecting yourself to do all of these perfectly would be its own barrier to being in a positive and harmonious vibrational state. Instead, congratulate yourself whenever you raise your vibrations, and continue to do so incrementally throughout your lifetime. And when you have a setback, laugh about it, learn from it, and continue to enjoy the process of your soul's unfolding.

DRINK LOTS OF WATER

Much has been said about the health benefits of drinking plenty of pure, clear water throughout the day, but the spiritual and energetic benefits are impressive as well. Water is one of the four natural elements and the one found in the most abundance in our bodies. When we move fresh water through our system, it's like a rainstorm in the forest: it makes everything fresh, clean, and vital, and it has the relentlessly cleansing effect of freshly melted snow rushing and tumbling through a canyon to form a clear mountain stream.

As we've seen, unicorns are famous for their ability to purify water, so before you drink, call on one or both of your unicorn guides to bless your water and attune it to the highest and most positive possible frequency.

Be sure to attend to your water's purity on the physical level as well. In most parts of the world (including the US), it's generally not a good idea to consume large amounts of tap water. So invest in your health with a water distiller or reverse osmosis filter, or purchase purified drinking water from a grocery store or water delivery service.

EAT CLEAN

When you realize that everything is vibration, it becomes clear that what we consume can't help but effect our personal vibration in the process. We are, after all, literally putting it into our bodies. Here are the two main ways to ensure what you're eating is supporting both your physical health and your vibrational well-being:

Avoid or minimize animal products. Unicorns (like their close relatives horses and deer) are vegetarians. It's also been said that they consciously avoid harming even the tiniest insect or spider. As someone who feels drawn to the realm of the unicorn, it's likely that you, especially, will benefit spiritually and emotionally from a kind diet and lifestyle. Kind living has a lighter and gentler vibration as it allows you to avoid consuming the vibrations of cruelty, exploitation, imprisonment, suffering, and pain. Of course, everyone's body is different, so no diet is one-size-fits-all: if you feel it's important for you to consume eggs, dairy, or meat, you're likely to feel better on many levels if you do so sparingly and select your sources consciously. Look for companies that treat animals as respectfully and lovingly as possible.

Eat lots of whole, organic fruits, vegetables, nuts, grains, and beans. If, like the unicorn, your entire diet is basically made up of whole, organic plant foods—and you go extra heavy on the fruits and vegetables—your vibration will thank you. You'll feel a consistent flow of calm, joyful, buoyant energy, and people and unicorns alike will be naturally drawn to your radiant glow.

MEDITATE

When it comes to raising your vibration, there is nothing quite like meditating every day—or at least five times per week. Regular meditation shifts your brain waves in ways that bring greater clarity, increased harmony, and enhanced ability to access the fullness of your intelligence, intuition, and creative genius. And contrary to popular belief, meditation need not be boring! In fact, all three of the unicorn portal key exercises you've done up to this point have been forms of meditation. The important thing when it comes to meditating is simply to do it. So find something you like and fit it into your schedule. There are plenty of guided meditations on YouTube as well as free meditation apps (such as Insight Timer, Headspace, and Calm) to help you find a guided meditation or meditation method you adore. And even five minutes a day can have a hugely positive effect!

TAKE SALT BATHS

A long soak in warm water containing sea salt, Epsom salt, or Himalayan pink salt is a deep cleanse for body, mind, and spirit. Salt baths are a powerful way to remove energetic debris, clear and activate your chakras (as mentioned above, these are the energy centers along the midline of your body), and purify your entire auric field. Before you soak, light a candle or two. Also be sure you have plenty of drinking water on hand so you stay hydrated.

LAUGH

As we discussed in the previous chapter, real, deep laughter instantly opens you up and transforms negative energy into positive energy. This is a potent form of vibration raising, so laugh often and laugh true.

ALIGN YOUR ACTIONS WITH YOUR VALUES

Finally, any time you change your behavior in a way that more authentically aligns your external actions with your internal values, you raise your overall vibration and consequently improve the quality of your life.

For example, as a person who cares about the survival and sustainability of the planet, incrementally moving toward a more loving treatment of the earth will incrementally raise your vibration. In other words, even one positive change, such as beginning to bring your own bags to the supermarket, switching to a more vegan or vegetarian diet, or starting a compost heap, will dial in a purer and more positive vibration for you. So look for little changes you can make that resonate with what you care about. Choose things that feel doable for you, and pace yourself.

[Isaac Newton] deduced that the white light that appears to surround us actually contains all the different colors we find in a rainbow. White was not separate from these colors—or a color unto itself—but was the result of all colors being reflected at once.

Joann Eckstut and Arielle Eckstut in
THE SECRET LANGUAGE OF COLOR

Living and Breathing
PURITY

To integrate all that you just read and to actualize it in your life experience, choose to perform at least three of the exercises below. For extra credit, do all six or do one of them more than once.

1   Find a water bottle you love. Drinking water is a sacred method of spiritual and energetic purification. Treat it as such by choosing a water bottle that speaks to your sense of wonder, beauty, and magic. Keep in mind that color, words, and imagery all affect the vibrations of the water. Listen to your intuition and choose accordingly.

2   Volunteer or donate to a worthy organization that protects the purity of water or just visit a local body of water and pick up trash. Unicorns are passionate about water purity. Express your unicorn-aligned devotion to the planet's well-being by helping to purify the world's oceans, rivers, and streams.

3   Meditate every day for the next seven days. Perhaps committing to a lifetime of meditation is a bit overwhelming, but seven days is a doable challenge. After that, you can always challenge yourself to do seven or fourteen or twenty-one more.

4   Eat only (or mostly) whole plant foods for the next seven days. As with meditation, you might feel more comfortable trying out the clean eating thing for seven days rather than indefinitely. It's short enough to be doable but long enough to begin to feel the astounding physical and vibrational benefits. You can find free vegan meal plans at forksoverknives.com.

5   Brainstorm ways you can more closely align your behavior with your values. First, make a list of the things you care about. Then examine that list thoughtfully and ask yourself: What changes can I make in my daily habits that will help me more closely align with these values? Whenever you think of something, write it down. When you've written down everything you can think of, identify the change that feels the easiest for you to put into practice right away and commit to making it. (There's no reason for this to be an opportunity to judge or criticize yourself: we all have room for positive change.)

6 Draw a warm bath. Light a white soy or vegetable wax candle. Dissolve two cups of Epsom salt in the water. Call on both unicorn guides to bless the water with vibrations of healing, purification, and love. Then soak for at least forty minutes. (Be sure to stay hydrated by drinking plenty of water as you soak.)

*Like the other unicorns, Uni
had a special swirly horn with
the power to heal and mend.*

Amy Krouse Rosenthal in
UNI THE UNICORN

four

HEALING

We have now examined three powerful energies the unicorn brings into our lives: wonder, alchemy, and purity. Considering these energies, it becomes obvious that aligning with the realm of the unicorn is a potent multidimensional healing tonic. Wonder heals our mental and emotional health. Alchemy brings divine harmony to body, mind, and spirit. And purity lifts, dissolves, and cleanses away anything standing in the way of our natural state, which is one of vibrant wellness and holistic vitality.

Furthermore, wherever you are on the spectrum of wellness, the unicorn reminds you that you have the power to heal yourself. This doesn't mean you'll never again benefit from a doctor's appointment or a visit to any other kind of mental or physical health professional. It simply means you have the intrinsic wisdom to change your own health for the better, which includes receiving clear intuitive guidance about changes to make and actions to take, including seeking professional support when it will be helpful.

It also means that you have the power to shift your personal energy in ways that bring about holistic healing from within. Once you awaken to these powers and abilities, you'll find that they allow you to heal others as well.

The Body Electric

The state of your body's energy flow—its clarity, potency, and consistency—has everything to do with the state of your physical health.

And energy is not just a metaphor: your body is literally electric. Can you feel electricity pulsing through you—throughout your organs, along the branching patterns of your nerves, and all the way to your fingers, toes, lips, and the top of your head? Can you feel your breath stoking its potency? If not, stop reading for a moment so you can close your eyes and notice your breath. Notice what your body is feeling. If you notice tension, soften it and send breath to it. Can you feel your weight on the earth? Can you feel the air on your skin? Can you feel the breath moving in and out of your belly? A simple awareness of your body is the first step in feeling energy flow.

In turn, becoming conscious of the feeling of energy within you is the first step toward being able to shift it in ways that bring healing, and shift it you can. After all, your brain is an incomprehensibly complex and powerful electrical instrument, and it is the undisputed master of your entire body's electrical flow.

Would you like to begin? A wonderful place to start is by consciously clearing and balancing the rainbow-colored wheels of energy that lie along your spinal column. We call these energy centers "chakras."

Shipshape Chakras

As we learned in the alchemy chapter, it really is all unicorns and rainbows. Case in point: the chakras, which illustrate that we are, each of us, a rainbow.

Nerve endings are present throughout your body, but, like aspens or wild poppies, they populate certain areas more abundantly than others. In particular, there are seven areas along your spinal column where these electrical nerve endings plentifully cluster, resulting in extra-electrical, extra-sensitive patches of energy in your body and aura, or energy field. These are the chakras. *Chakra* translates to "wheel," and indeed, chakras are generally imagined as rapidly spinning wheels of energy and light.

The first chakra is at the base of the spine, and the seventh is at the crown of the head. Like notes on a scale—or, even more precisely like a rainbow—the vibratory rates of each chakra ascend, causing them to appear as red (at the base), orange, yellow, green, blue, indigo, and violet or white (at the crown).

In addition to colors and areas of the body, each chakra corresponds with areas of your life, as well as aspects of your physical and psychological well-being. This makes the chakra system a useful roadmap for energy work of all varieties, as well as a handy diagnostic and calibration tool for holistic health.

If it all sounds too complex or intimidating, relax! While you can certainly continue to learn about the chakra system for a lifetime, you can begin to tune into and work with your chakras right away, and you will immediately notice positive results. In fact, working with them directly is the best teacher: over time, your understanding of them will absolutely become more masterful and nuanced.

The chakras are as follows:

THE ROOT CHAKRA is located at the base of the spine, or the area where your body touches the earth when you're sitting with your spine straight. Its color is ruby red. When it's healthy, you feel grounded, nourished, and supported by Mother Earth. You feel safe in the physical world, and you have a healthy relationship with money and material resources.

THE SACRAL CHAKRA is located at your lower belly or womb area, just below your belly button. Its color is citrine orange. When it's healthy, you enjoy your desires and express them in balanced ways. You feel natural about desiring food, sex, and other sensory pleasures, and you feel playful, creative, and free to be yourself.

THE SOLAR PLEXUS CHAKRA is located at your stomach area, above your belly button and below your sternum and rib cage. Its color is sunshine yellow. When it's healthy, you feel strong and are comfortable expressing your power in loving and balanced ways. You feel wonderfully able to act in accordance with an intrinsic sense of purpose and to shape the world according to your intention and will.

THE HEART CHAKRA is located in the center of your sternum: the emotional center—the place that feels both love and grief. Its color is emerald or jade green. When it's healthy, you feel loved and lovable. You feel safe to embody the tender openness of love and to both receive that love and express it in authentic and satisfying ways.

THE THROAT CHAKRA is located in the center of your neck. Its color is sky blue. When it's healthy, your words are naturally aligned with your feelings and you express yourself clearly, lovingly, and effectively. Your spoken and written words, as well as your emotions and creative outlets, flow from you in a balanced and beautiful way.

THE THIRD EYE CHAKRA is located in the center of your forehead, just above the center point of your eyebrows. Its color is indigo. When it's healthy, you see into the heart of reality: beyond the physical form or the spoken words. You see the truth, which allows you to perceive emotions, root causes, patterns, solutions, and potentialities in deep and accurate ways.

THE CROWN CHAKRA is located at the top of your head, where a round skylight would be if you wanted to let in the sun. Its color is violet or white. When it's healthy, you feel connected to and one with All That Is. You feel as if your life is naturally guided and constantly illuminated by divine light. You have a perspective that allows you to transcend this temporary reality and see into the heart of eternity.

Please note that while the root chakra and crown chakra both spin horizontally, like ceiling fans, the middle five chakras spin vertically, like box fans.

UNICORN PORTAL KEY #4:

Be a Rainbow

This key is made of shimmering gold. Along its length appear seven radiant gems in every color of the rainbow, spinning and sparkling with a bright light from within.

Sit comfortably with your spine straight, perhaps in front of your unicorn altar, outside in a serene natural setting, or somewhere else where you won't be disturbed.

Close your eyes and become conscious of your breath. Notice as it goes in and out, and allow it to naturally deepen. Notice any tension in your body. Send breath to it and allow it to soften, open, and relax. Settle into your body and feel your weight gently anchoring you to the earth.

Remember that wherever you are now is sacred. Whether you are indoors or out, in a city or rural area, the land beneath you is none other than Mother Earth, and every inch of her surface is hallowed ground and a potential vortex of power.

As you remember this, notice that you are encompassed within the trunk of a giant interdimensional tree. Roots of light go deep into the earth beneath you, and a trunk and branches of light reach high into the sky. This is the Tree of Life, and her roots are bathed in the golden-white light at the core of Mother Earth. Her branches are drinking in the diamond-white light of infinity as they stretch out of the atmosphere and into outer space.

See or sense this bright golden-white light at the earth's core moving up the trunk and into the ruby-red fan at the base of your spine that is your root chakra. As this light enters your root chakra, the chakra spins more quickly. This allows it to spin off any stuck, heavy, or challenging energy so that it becomes an even brighter and more vibrant red than before. Breathe deeply as you continue to bathe this chakra in the golden-white light from Mother Earth.

Now see the light move up to your sacral chakra, the spinning wheel of orange light in your lower belly area. See this chakra bathed in light and sense that it spins faster, spinning off any energetic debris. Breathe deeply and allow this chakra to be cleansed and balanced in the light.

Next, the light enters your solar plexus chakra, the wheel of sunshine-yellow light just above your belly button and below your sternum. Allow this chakra to be similarly cleansed and balanced in the light as you continue to breathe deeply and steadily.

The light from Mother Earth now enters your heart chakra, the emerald-green wheel of radiant light at the emotional center in the middle of your sternum area. Breathe deeply and allow this chakra to be bathed in light. See it spin faster and become brighter and more vital.

The light from the core of the earth next enters your throat chakra, the spinning wheel of sky-blue light in the center of your neck area. Sense the blue becoming brighter and the wheel of light spinning faster as it is bathed in the light.

The light now enters your third eye chakra, the indigo circle of spinning light on your forehead, just above the center of your eyebrows. Breathe deeply and steadily as this area is cleansed, activated, and balanced.

And now your crown chakra—the spinning circle of violet or white light at the top of your head—is bathed in the light from Mother Earth. It becomes brighter and spins faster as you breathe deeply and allow it to be cleansed.

Now become aware of the trunk of light above your head, reaching high into the heavens and out of the earth's atmosphere. Sense the branches reaching into space and the cosmos, and sense them drinking in diamond-white light that spills down through the trunk, into the top of your head, and throughout all your chakras like a shimmering internal fountain or waterfall of cleansing illumination. Breathe and relax as you feel all your chakras and your entire energy field refreshed and enlivened with this cosmic light from above.

Finally, become aware of the golden-white earth light mixing with the diamond-white cosmic light to create a swirl of sparkling, blindingly bright, daisy-toned, white-and-golden light that fills your entire body and aura, and extends outward to encompass you in a sphere of light. See or sense this sphere gently rotating in a clockwise direction around you to seal in the positivity. Set the intention that within this sphere only love remains, and through this sphere only love may enter. Give thanks to Mother Earth and Father Sky.

When you feel ready, become conscious of your weight on the earth once again. Come back into the place where you are sitting. Open your eyes.

The rainbow key is now yours. Add it to your key ring of energy and light.

A Light from the Shadows

Many of us (including myself) were abused as children or adolescents: sexually, physically, and/or emotionally. Still others were abused as adults. But whether or not we were abused, every single one of us has experienced trauma at some point in the past: things that hurt us, scared us, caused us to feel lonely, and generally broke our hearts. When this trauma isn't acknowledged, processed fully, or dealt with in a healthy way, it becomes lodged in our emotions and energy field, and it holds us back from the vibrant wellness of mind, body, and spirit that is our birthright and natural state.

Luckily, the unicorn realm to which you are currently acclimating yourself specializes in helping us locate these old areas of pain so we can feel them, heal them, and let them go. Once we do that, we free up trapped energy and become even stronger, wiser, and healthier than we otherwise could have been. Indeed, the unicorn confirms that the bumper-sticker wisdom is solid: It's never too late to have a happy childhood.

As mentioned above, your mind, body, and spirit are interconnected and interwoven. It's actually even truer to say that there is no separation between them. This means that one way to discover old, unhealed emotional pain from your past is to assess and examine any areas of your physical body experiencing health challenges. Another is to identify aspects of your body that you do not currently feel comfortable with for any reason.

In your journal or notebook, make a list of any health issues you are currently experiencing. Include both temporary challenges and more longstanding ones. Include illnesses of any kind, injuries big or small, allergies, reactions, sensitivities, conditions, recurring challenges (such as headaches), and syndromes. Even if you haven't been able to figure out exactly what something is called or why you're experiencing it (such as chronic digestive issues with no apparent explanation), write it down. And even if it's just a fleabite, if it's bothering you, write it down.

Remember: everything is connected. Our external experience is always a manifestation of something on the internal realm. That's why, even if you think you know the reason for a challenge (for example, if you find yourself saying something like "debilitating menstrual cramps are not emotional, they're genetic" or "my bruised toe has nothing to do with my past, it just has to do with the fact that I stubbed it on a rock"), it's important that you write it down anyway.

Next, make a list of any areas of your body that you don't love or that you repeatedly feel ashamed or critical of. Don't add insult to injury by judging yourself if this list is long. Instead, feel excited every time you think of something to put on the list. After all, the more you write down, the more healing potential you have, and the more energy you have available to be freed up.

Finally, make a list of any area of your health or physical body that could use a bit of attention or healing. For example, maybe your stomach is often tense, your shoulders sometimes ache, or you'd like to feel your lungs have a bit more capacity when you find yourself walking up a hill.

Once you've completed your list, you might want to sit comfortably in front of your altar once more. Take some deep, conscious breaths and relax. Now spend a bit of time with each item you wrote down. Make it its own heading in your journal. Then tune into the area of your body where this challenge manifests. What does this area of your body have to tell you about this challenge? What feelings are associated with it? Don't rush this process. Give your body time to relax and open up to you. Do you see any pictures, memories, relationships, patterns, or life conditions associated with the pain, discomfort, or body part? Can you translate what your body is telling you by manifesting this challenge? If not, what if you had to guess?

Be sure to consider the quality of the feeling. For example, if burns, where have you felt emotionally burned? If it itches, what is irritating you? If it feels like pressure, who or what is bearing down on you?

Once you've taken a quiet moment to settle into your body and tune into the issue on a deep level, what you are sensing (or guessing) without censoring or intellectualizing?

As I alluded to above, you may assume a challenge is purely and unavoidably genetic, such as debilitating menstrual cramps when your mom and your mom's mom both experienced them too. But that may not be the case or it may be only a part of the whole story. Rather, they could stem from a deeply rooted emotional challenge that has been present throughout generations and passed down all along the way. For example, painful menstrual cramps often manifest in women who do not feel 100 percent comfortable being women. Somewhere along the way, they absorbed the unfortunate cultural message that being female made them weak, silly, or otherwise inferior. And this happened on such a deep level that they didn't quite realize it and were therefore unable to process it emotionally. The very feminine process of menstruating, then, took the brunt of their emotional pain by becoming intensely physically painful. If your mother was one of these women, you could have learned these emotional and physical patterns from her, who had learned them from *her* mother, and so on.

By bringing the inner source of such a challenge out into the open, you give yourself the unique opportunity to heal it in all directions of time, not only for you, but also for your family line. After all, as Einstein pointed out, "Time is an illusion." Within this illusion of time, when you heal yourself, your descendants as well as your ancestors all have the opportunity to experience this healing.

Here are some further clues to what your body may be telling you through your current physical challenges:

- ❋ Your feet represent your understanding of life and what is currently happening in your life.
- ❋ Your legs represent your ability to move forward in any area of life.
- ❋ Your knees represent change.
- ❋ Your hips represent your ability to move through life easily and gracefully.
- ❋ Your womb and reproductive system represent your gender identity as well as your creativity and the healthy expression of your physical desires.
- ❋ Your bladder and urinary tract represent your degree of peace and harmony with life, as well as being true to what feels right to you sexually and your degree of trust of your sexual partner(s).

* Your belly and digestive system
  represent your ability to process and
  digest ideas and experiences.

* Your lungs represent your ability to be
  nourished by life and the present moment.

* Your heart represents your
  authenticity, your life purpose, and
  your ability to love and be loved.

* Your breasts represent your ability to nourish
  the people and creations you care about.

* Your arms represent being open to
  life and holding on to the things
  and people you care about.

* Your hands represent your ability to
  craft your life and express mastery in
  your chosen art(s) and profession.

* Your shoulders represent what you
  are carrying and the responsibilities
  you have chosen to adopt.

* Your neck represents being open and
  flexible to fresh perspectives.

* Your throat represents your voice and your
  comfort with speaking your truth with love.

* Your mouth represents your ability
  to take in nourishment, make
  decisions, and attract prosperity.

* Your nose and nasal passages
  represent your intuition, personal
  power, and sense of self-esteem.
* Your ears represent your ability to
  listen deeply and to hear the truth
  within, between, and beyond words.
* Your eyes represent your ability to see yourself
  and your life conditions clearly and with love.
* Your brain represents the patterns and
  programs you are running and the
  stories you tell yourself about who
  you are and why you are here.
* Your skin represents your sense of
  cleanliness, worthiness, and safety.

Take your time and enjoy the process of detective work. Continue until you have some solid working hypotheses about the inner emotional causes for each health challenge.

Next, it's time for miracles.

Deep within [the] architecture
[of your soul] lie seven precious
jewels, spinning in colorful splendor.
These jewels are sacred centers of
transformation, stepping stones on the
journey of healing and awakening.

Anodea Judith in
CHAKRAS

Conjuring Miracles

Let's conjure up a miracle.

Choose the health issue that challenges you the most. If you don't have any pressing issues right now, choose something from your list for the purpose of this exercise. Look back in your journal to examine what you've discovered and written about this challenge. Then light a white candle on your unicorn altar. Take a moment to close your eyes, take some deep breaths, and call on your unicorn guides for intuitive guidance and energetic support. Then write a prescription for healing by following these steps:

If there are limiting beliefs associated with this challenge, revise them and write them down as positive affirmations. For example, "Women are silly" could become "I now embrace my feminine qualities of strength and intelligence." "Life is scary and uncertain" could become "Life supports me in all ways. I am safe." "I am destined to be broke" could become "I am tapped into a steady flow of cash and ever-increasing wealth."

For each affirmation you wrote, think of three ways it could be truer than your original limiting belief. For example, for "I now embrace my feminine qualities of strength and intelligence," you might find three examples of feminine people who also are (or were) strong and intelligent:

let's say Hedy Lamarr, Margaret Atwood, and Michelle Obama. For "Life supports me in all ways. I am safe," you might think of three people, occurrences, or situations that support you now or have supported you in the past. For "I am tapped into a steady flow of cash and ever-increasing wealth," you may make a note of just how many opportunities there are in the world, write down an example of someone who is continually prospering (if they can, why can't you?), and bring to mind some of the most memorable boons and blessings you've received in the past.

Come up with one or more concrete changes you can make or actions you can take that will support your physical healing. Now that your intuition is tuned in deeply to the full dynamic of the health issue, and now that you've fueled your outer healing with some powerful inner shifts, notice what guidance and pictures you receive about what changes or actions will help shift the physical challenge. For example, you might receive the message to drink more water, exercise regularly, make an appointment with a dentist, stop eating dairy, or meditate regularly. You might even feel guided to do something seemingly unrelated like clear clutter, sing more often, or make more friends at work.

Release the issue to the light of the sun and moon. Close your eyes and settle your mind once again. Take some deep breaths. Call on your solar unicorn guide to fill and surround you with the golden light of the sun. Relax and willingly offer up the health issue to the light of the sun. Feel it burning away and being purified, cleansed, and perfectly transmuted in precisely the way that will heal you. Then call on your lunar unicorn guide to fill and surround you with the silvery light of the moon. Relax and willingly surrender the health issue to the moon's light. Feel it being soothed, cooled, balanced, and completely dissolved. Give thanks to the sun, moon, and your unicorn guides.

Post or place your affirmations somewhere where you will remember to say them every morning and evening while looking in the mirror. Also commit to making the changes or taking the actions your intuition indicated will help with your physical healing.

Over the days and weeks to follow, notice how the issue improves. Be alert to any additional intuitive guidance or insights you may receive.

You can repeat this process any time you'd like to engender a healing miracle for yourself.

The spiral shape [of the unicorn's horn] symbolizes the spiraling pattern of life energy, recognized by metaphysicians from ancient times until the present. Spiritually, the spiral signifies movement from the secret depths of your center outward into the world at large——and back again.

Skye Alexander in
UNICORNS

Living and Breathing
HEALING

To integrate all that you just read and to actualize it in your life experience, choose to perform at least three of the exercises below. For extra credit, do all six or do one of them more than once.

1   Repeat the chakra meditation from the "be a rainbow" portal key in this chapter every day for the next seven days. After that, stay in the habit or perform it anytime you feel you could use an energetic tune-up.

2   If one of the chakras seems to be particularly pertinent for you right now, work with its accompanying color in meditation and visualization. Regularly envision yourself filled and cocooned within the color in the form of blindingly bright light.

3   If you were abused as a child or adolescent, ask yourself if you have properly processed the pain and anger of that occurrence. If not, take time to do so. Be aware that children and adolescents are never properly equipped to place blame where blame is due, and

therefore in all cases turn their natural response of anger upon themselves. As adults, we are finally able to realize that we did not do anything to deserve either the abuse or the anger we previously directed at ourselves. This necessitates redirecting anger toward those who abused us and those whom we may feel did not adequately protect us. We must do this before we can properly forgive. Otherwise, the old wounds continue to fester. It hurts and it's messy to go through this realization and redirection, but until survivors of abuse do it, we continue to suffer emotionally, mentally, and physically.

4   Create artwork depicting one or more of the affirmations you composed. Display it where you'll see it often.

5   Throughout the day, regularly bring your attention to your breath. Allow it to naturally deepen as you keep your awareness on the in-breath and the out-breath. Then notice where you are holding tension in your body. Send breath to those areas and consciously relax them. In this way, you will get in the habit of letting energy flow freely through your body while also learning to become more aware of the quality of your personal energy.

6 Take a reverent and meditative walk in nature. This always refuels, rebalances, and recalibrates your energy field, and it therefore enhances every aspect of your holistic health and well-being.

Your unicorn's devotion
is limitless.

Joules Taylor in
THE WISDOM OF UNICORNS

five

DEVOTION

While devotion is not a quality we hear frequently lauded in the West, it's a magnificent quality indeed—one that has the potential to infuse our lives with great meaning, inspiration, and joy.

When we do talk about devotion in the Western world, it's most often devotion to one's spouse, one's children, or a charitable cause. These are noble devotions all.

But the devotion the unicorn calls for us to cultivate is devotion to beauty in all its many forms. This includes:

* the beauty of the planet: the fresh air,
  the blue sky, vibrantly healthy animals,
  and lush green growing things

* the beauty of the universe: our
  concept of infinity, the bright light
  of divinity, and pure potentiality

* the beauty of the human spirit:
  friendship, love, laughter, connection,
  creativity, understanding, our natural
  desire to help others, and our constant
  drive to establish peace on earth

* the beauty of the present moment:
  creating and enjoying the beauty in the
  little things within and around us in
  this one sacred moment we call now

In Hinduism, choosing a deity to honor above all others makes you a devotee of that deity. Priests and priestesses of various spiritualities—those who have dedicated their lives to a particular spiritual path—are also often called "devotees."

We of the unicorn clan are also devotees. We are devotees of beauty.

Everyday Sacred

So much of our time is spent doing things that are not commonly considered sublime, transcendent, or even mildly enjoyable: cleaning the house, brushing our teeth, parallel parking, waiting in line at the bank. But being a devotee makes it possible for us to transform everything we do—even the tiniest or most mundane of tasks—into something that brings more beauty into the world.

Cleaning the house becomes an act of creating paradise on earth.

Brushing our teeth becomes an act of honoring the smile with which we shine light and love into the world.

Parallel parking becomes an act of precision, focus, and presence.

Waiting in line at the bank becomes an act of emanating peaceful energy and prosperous wishes to our fellow human beings.

Will we forget sometimes and lose our temper, get impatient, fail to focus, or become beleaguered by boredom? Of course! Devotees are not perfect. They are just devoted. Like athletes devoted to a sport, that means showing up regularly, practicing, falling down, getting up, trying again, and doing our best.

We are all telling ourselves stories all the time anyway: about what is important, what we should care about, and why we are doing things. Claiming our identity as devotees of beauty allows us to tell a story that weaves our daily life into a tapestry of conscious, compassionate continuity. It allows us to measure our values by the axiom *Above all else, beauty.* Above all else, true, eminent beauty: the beauty of the planet, the universe, the human spirit, and the present moment. Is what I am doing serving and magnifying that beauty? If not, is it possible to shift the intention and feeling behind it so that it is serving and magnifying that beauty? We can then let those things that are not in alignment with beauty—actions, intentions, beliefs, relationships, habits, values, and commitments—fall away. We can release them with love and send them on their way.

You Are Meant to Shine

In the past, when you have done things out of fear, you have believed that it mattered how stylish or famous or cool you were, not in your own heart or for your own pleasure, but in the eyes and opinions of others. You have believed that you needed to look like someone other than yourself in order to be beautiful or respected or loved. You have believed that in order to survive and thrive, you needed to ignore some of the deepest truths of your heart.

This wasn't because you were malicious or ignorant or self-absorbed. Of course it wasn't! It was because you were afraid and because you were hypnotized by stories you were told by the media, your culture, and even possibly your family. But all along, deep down, you knew the truth, just as you know it now: you are glorious and wise. You are beautiful just as you are. You are worthy of love just for being you. You need only follow the noblest desires of your heart, which are also the truest ones and which counsel you to offer your gifts to the world out of the joy of giving, creating beauty, magnifying love, and being of service. There is no need to pretend otherwise any longer.

The following exercise will help you to clearly release what is false in favor of what is true. This will allow you to shine brightly, live authentically, and heartily devote your life to creating and magnifying beauty in its truest expression.

UNICORN PORTAL KEY #5:

Shine like the Sun

The Shinto goddess of the sun, Amaterasu, whose name means "shining in the heaven," once retreated to a cave, depriving the world of her light. Upon being presented with the gift of a sacred mirror, she glimpsed her own true beauty and emerged from the cave to bless the world with her life-giving radiance once again.

This key is a gift from Amaterasu, who wants you to know that you possess the sun's same radiance within your very being. While it, like the others, is shaped as a key, it also resembles a tiny golden hand mirror with a reflective circle at its base, which constantly reflects the blinding golden-white light that is your true self.

Near your unicorn altar or somewhere else quiet, where you won't be disturbed, sit comfortably with your spine straight. Close your eyes and take some deep, conscious breaths. Let go of the past. Let go of the future. Let go of all human storylines and timelines and just be here now, in the cradle of the radiant present.

In your mind's eye, find yourself in a cave. The cave is warm and dark and safe. Within it, you feel at peace because it gives you a buffer from the world of human relationships and stories, which has been draining you of your enthusiasm and hurting you with its criticism, harshness, and frenetic activity. Relax here and decompress from all of this. Let yourself feel safe and cocooned within this deep, hidden, solitary cave.

After you feel sufficiently relaxed and recharged, you begin to notice another feeling: loneliness. You, like all humans, have an inborn need to connect with other humans: to enjoy their light and to feel that they are enjoying yours. You realize that you can't spend your entire life hiding out in this cave because you crave the joy of connecting with other people in satisfying, nourishing ways that allow you to share your unique perspectives, talents, and gifts with the world.

This poses a problem: you want to connect with others, but you don't want your heart to feel consistently battered and hurt by the world. You also don't want to feel judged or compared or socially drained or pressured to do things you don't want to do in order to survive or be accepted.

At a loss as to how to proceed, you mentally summon first your solar unicorn guide, then your lunar. After each appears in the cave with you—the solar on your right and the lunar on your left—you mentally ask: "What do I do now? I don't want to stay in the cave, but I don't want to come out either."

Your guides tilt their heads toward each other and direct energy through their horns to create a sacred mirror. You look into it and see yourself as pure, shining, and beautiful. This is your true divine self, and you are mesmerized by your own authentic beauty, which comes from within. You also see clearly that you are a loving soul who dearly loves bringing beauty, magic, and healing into the world for the benefit and joy of all.

Seeing this divine reflection locks you into your true frequency as a powerful being of love and light. When you consider reentering the human realm, you see clearly and feel passionately that you can easily exist in this realm as the truth of who you are, and that you can happily let all else fall away. Even if you may perceive the old cultural, media, or family stories, you can learn to relate to them in such a way that you don't give them energy or make decisions based on them ever again.

The present moment is all there is. Love is all that matters. Claiming your role as a devotee of beauty will illuminate the path before you so that you can connect with the world in a way that feels divine.

If it feels right, take some time to examine what this might look like in terms of decisions, values, goals, actions, motivations, and everyday habits.

Thank your unicorn guides heartily. Offer a red apple to your solar guide and a pale yellow apple to your lunar guide.

Notice the sacred mirror in miniature, hovering in front of you in the form of a key. Gently take it and place it on your etheric key ring.

Feel your gravity on the earth beneath you, and gradually come out of the cave and back into the human world.

Paradise Is Here

In New Age spirituality and psychology, attention is often paid to identifying and analyzing what is wrong: what limiting beliefs, fears, or past hurts are holding us back. And this can certainly be helpful! There are times when it is undeniably appropriate. But what we don't always remember to consider is that we are not just held back by unexamined challenges; we are also held back by the enormity of the beauty that surrounds us at all times. We are held back by it because it scares us. It is, in fact, so staggering in its scope that we cannot comprehend it. And when we try to, it hurts us.

Have you ever been so struck by how much you love someone that your heart ached? Have you ever adopted an animal and loved that animal so much you were terrified of something happening to it? Has the beauty of a natural setting or a work of art ever overwhelmed you to the point of tears? If so, you know a thing or two about the pain involved with allowing yourself to perceive the beauty and magic of it all.

In fact, the beauty of this planet and our human existence is so vast, so unfathomable, and so heartbreaking in its immensity that we make up stories to try to contain and limit it. We tell ourselves (or allow ourselves to be told) things like life is hard; life isn't fair; it's us versus them; if something can go wrong, it will go wrong; I hate Mondays; a good man is hard to find; and I may not like it, but this is the way things have to be.

Walking the path of the beauty devotee, then, asks us to become ever braver as we open our eyes and our hearts wider and wider to the truth: life is beautiful. Extremely, extravagantly, excruciatingly beautiful. And also precious. And transient. And fragile.

A quick way to get there is to think of lying on your deathbed. You are about to die, and you know it. As you look back on your life, you can see that even the moments you thought of as boring, run-of-the-mill, or insignif-icant—maybe even especially those moments—were imbued with so much exquisiteness, so much splendor, so much delight, it's actually ridiculous. From this vantage point, it's easy to treasure the experiences that you will be bidding farewell to forever in this lifetime: the vast blue openness of the sky; the golden-white sunlight on your face; the savory scent of popcorn popping; the mellifluous sound of a loved one laughing.

It might not be perfect, but it's paradise, this life. And it's all around you right now. In fact, now is the only time you can enjoy it because now is the only time there is. If you miss now, you miss everything.

Much like glimpsing a unicorn in the woods, we must become quiet, attentive, and still if we are to perceive the precious beauty of life itself. Furthermore, in both cases, we must be brave.

To cultivate this present-moment bravery, daily mindfulness meditation is of the essence. To practice it, begin by sitting comfortably in front of your unicorn altar or anywhere else quiet and relaxing. Sit with your spine straight in a comfortable way. Set a timer for five minutes. Then close your eyes and simply notice the movement of your breath. When you breathe in, notice you are breathing in. When you breathe out, notice you are breathing out. If it helps, you can think "in, out" as you breathe. When you notice your mind has wandered (and you will), simply bring it back. It's not a failure. It's simply part of the process, because minds wander: it's what minds do. Repeat daily. Over time, if you like, you can build up to ten or twenty minutes, but just five minutes a day is great too.

Keep in mind that many people want to practice daily meditation but don't keep up the habit. Why? Though they probably blame the boredom, the real reason is the beauty. It's too much for most people. When you notice your breath, you go deep. First, you touch on old pain you never let yourself feel. Then, after you move through that (if you keep meditating by paying attention to your breath daily), you start to feel overwhelmed by the crushing beauty of life . . . and, to be honest, it's likely that at times you also will be overwhelmed by boredom. But boredom is just a defense mechanism to protect us from the pain of the beauty, and meditation helps us break through.

If you don't want to feel the beauty because it's so painful or because it's so boring before you break through, you won't. It's as simple as that. The beauty will still be there, but you will escape it and it will escape you. That is your right; you have the free will that allows you to do that.

So. Will you get, and then stay, in the habit of meditating? Well, would you like to be a devotee of beauty? Would you like to appreciate the beauty now, before you are on your deathbed? Are you committed to the path—indeed, devoted to it—as devotees must be? Then you must. You must be brave. You must keep on showing up for meditation, which means going deep, breaking through boredom, cracking open your heart, and feeling it all.

Of course, like getting into any good habit, you might skip a day or a week or even a month here and there. Don't use that as an excuse to give up. However long it's been, show up again and again and again, until it feels as natural and as needed as taking a shower or brushing your teeth.

Noticing the paradise that surrounds you also requires you to come into the present moment during times when you aren't meditating. Breath meditation helps with that also, because you can use the same mechanism to bring your awareness back to your breath throughout your day, which aligns mind, body, and spirit and allows you to come into harmonious oneness with the utter gorgeousness of life.

Hidden and Wild

You are drawn to the realm of the unicorn for many reasons, including this one: you identify with the unicorn's natural desire to exist in the pristine, secreted forest, safely tucked away from the ways of humans and the modern world. In many ways, you share their habit of only showing themselves to those whom they sense they can trust, to those who are pure of heart.

At times this has caused pain for you because you have felt as if you didn't fit in here on earth or even as if you didn't want to be here. While a misty forest, a rainbow waterfall, or a sunlit glade may have sounded just about right, they're a world away from a city street, a room full of strangers, or a bustling shopping mall.

Here's the good news: much like a unicorn, you can remain hidden and wild, even while dwelling in plain sight in the domesticated human world. Not only is this a possibility, it's a recommendation.

If it sounds like I'm talking in riddles, here is what I mean: being a devotee of beauty and an initiate to the realm of the unicorn is not something every human is currently ready to understand or embrace. For example, some will see this book and scoff at it as silly or frivolous or delusional. For many people currently dwelling on this planet, the very word "unicorn" is enough to draw a smirk. We don't need to rage at these people or resent them or try to convert them to our point of view. It's not our business what they think of the books we read or the thoughts we think or the feelings we feel. It's only our business to be devotees of beauty, which means that we will know them to be the divine, bright, beautiful beings they are in truth. Their opinions and preferences, like everyone's, are just temporary clouds floating over the infinite clear blue sky of who they really are.

When we come from a place of love and acceptance while not feeling like we need to disclose everything about us right away to everyone we meet, we are dwelling in the realm of truth, where there is no separation: we are actually one with all beings and All That Is. The more time we spend with someone, the more we will have a sense of what, when, and how we are ready to share the perspectives and practices that are important to us. Maybe we never will! Or maybe we will be surprised to find out that our friend or acquaintance is not actually that different from us after all. With watchful gentleness and patience, we will know precisely what to do.

Of course, just because we are one with everyone, and just because everyone's true identity is divine beauty and light, it doesn't mean we need to hang out with everyone. Again, we can take our cue from the unicorn. If your intuition or natural preferences counsel you that it is not healthy or desirable for you to spend time with someone, or if a certain person drains your energy and leaves you feeling depressed or depleted, you will benefit from setting a boundary with this person by not spending time with them or offering them any of your time, energy, or attention.

Like a unicorn, be wise, gentle, loving, and patient, but also be fiercely protective of your right to run wild and free. Be fiercely protective of your creativity, your sensitivity, your wonder, and your joy. Express it all bravely and let it fuel your every action and intention, but don't go around telling everyone you meet (for example) about your unicorn guides and your etheric keys to the unicorn portal. In addition to containing the magic you are working in a way that will make it more effective for creating positive change within and around you, being discerning and keeping silent when appropriate are important aspects of your devotion to beauty. Specifically, they are ways of devoting yourself to protecting the wild beauty, magic, and power that dwell within you.

Passionate Service

We unicorn people are passionate about the well-being of Mother Earth and all our fellow earthlings. We hear the call to help, and we feel best when we follow it.

In our modern world, we are told that it is important to find a career path and excel at it, and doing such a thing is not wrong. But we will feel best when we place our focus on how we can best be of service to the world instead of on our own personal success. This is not only what we will feel best doing, it is what we will most excel at and what will bring healing and joy in the way only we can. It is not something other than a career path at which we excel; it is the same. It is simply a rearranging of the order of values.

Being of service can call to mind images like volunteering at a soup kitchen or doing social work with underprivileged children, and these can be excellent avenues of service. But if your passion and joy lie in hairdressing or painting or geology or real estate, this is a clue to your talents and a clue to the way you can best serve your fellow earthlings. Almost every profession, pastime, and activity is an opportunity to serve and to bring more beauty to the planet, provided you begin with the key ingredient: the authentic, heartfelt intention to serve the planet and to make it a more beautiful place to be.

Once you set that intention and begin to make decisions based on it, the universe will flood you with support, and you will find doors of opportunity appear everywhere, just like magic.

Here is an unspeakable secret:
Paradise is all around us and
we do not understand.

Thomas Merton in
CONJECTURES OF A GUILTY BYSTANDER

Living and Breathing
DEVOTION

To integrate all that you just read and to actualize it in your life experience, choose to perform at least three of the exercises below. For extra credit, do all six or do one of them more than once.

1   Create even more beauty in your home through clutter clearing, cleaning, organizing, and decorating. Even though you've already started this journey, perhaps you can take it even further: Is there another closet to clear, another shelf to dust, another nook to beautify? If not, can you do so in your car, your storage space, or your place of employment? Create beauty, order, harmony, and peace in your own space, which will emanate waves of grace to the world.

2   Find a beautiful natural setting and spend time there alone. Honor the beauty of the moment. Notice the colors, the scents, the patterns, the movements, and the sounds.

3   For one day, see how much beauty you can bring into the world. In every situation—wherever you are and whatever you're doing—ask yourself: What can I do to gift the world with beauty right now? Perhaps you can give a coworker flowers, give a cashier a compliment, or tape a five-dollar bill to the inside of a bathroom stall.

4   If you haven't already, begin the mindfulness habit. Set aside five minutes or more a day to notice your breath. Also bring your mind back to observing your breath whenever you think of it throughout the day.

5   Take action on you soul's desire for selfless service. During the unicorn portal key visualization in this chapter, you glimpsed your own radiance and saw your own authenticity. If there's a direction your soul feels joyful about taking in the realm of service (which also may be one and the same with your career), take action on it. One step is all you can take at a time anyway, so take a step. Do a web search, contact a college, get a journal for your writing project, or peruse art classes in your area. After you take one step, take another step, and then another.

6 Make three small changes in your habits that will better support the planet. Most of us are not perfect when it comes to being eco-friendly. Rather, most of us are doing our very best to steadily improve. With that in mind, what are three small changes you can make in your habits that will be in alignment with your devotion to the beauty of the planet? For example, cutting dairy out of your diet is wonderful for the planet, as is composting, walking or biking to work, and abstaining from using plastic bags. Choose three changes like these and take action on making them today.

*When those elements are ignited
by the spark that resides in the
heart of us all, it creates the sixth
element: the element of magic!*

Lauren Faust in
MY LITTLE PONY

six

MAGIC

Magic is supernatural.

Not in the sense that it is beyond what is natural, but in the sense that it is super-duper natural (i.e., extremely, incredibly, off-the-hook natural).

As a sensitive electrical being that is wired with a mind-bendingly complex system of nerves and impulses, it is natural for you to be able to sense and shape energy with the awesome power of your mind as you channel that power through your body, environment, and emotions.

As a vibrant component of the living, breathing planet we call our home, you possess the potent forces of the earth within your very being.

As a glittering jewel of uniqueness in a vast expanse of time and space, your ability to conceptualize infinity means infinity is within you. And if the theoretical physicists who say the universe is a hologram are right, you literally contain the blueprint to the whole incomprehensible shebang within your every cell.

Face it: you're super-duper, double-deluxe natural, and if you decide to work your magic in this little corner of infinity, nothing can stop you.

Working your magic means owning your power. It means knowing that your consciousness shapes your reality and that you can intentionally change your consciousness in order to change your reality. It means being the master of your own life and steering your own glittery rainbow ship on the magical sea of love.

So, my dear unicorn initiate, are you ready to work your magic?

No need to answer; the question is rhetorical. Of course you're ready. And when the student is ready, the teacher appears.

The Teacher Appearing

The teacher is not outside of you; the teacher is you. But your true identity is infinite intelligence, and your classroom (as both student and teacher) is this life experience. Do you think it's an accident that you have found this book and that you are reading these words? Do you think these words are coming from outside of you? Nothing is outside of you. Just as you dwell in infinity, infinity dwells within you, and neither makes any more sense than the other.

Perhaps you've heard it before, but it bears restating: you create your own reality. Your thoughts, beliefs, and expectations literally construct your world, through your perceptions as well as through what you create, manifest, and attract into your life experience. In accordance with the law of attraction, the more you believe this to be true, the truer it will be for you. (It should be noted that by not believing, you also construct your reality, albeit a reality in which it appears that you do not construct your reality.) Over time, the practice of magic will convince you more and more of your power, consequently freeing up more and more power for you to use.

How, then, do you learn to work magic? By doing. By trying. By showing up and doing your best. And where do you even start? Right where you are: on the sacred ground beneath your feet.

To prepare for your first magical working as an ally and initiate of the unicorn realm, find, gather, purchase, or otherwise obtain a simple representation of the first four natural elements: earth, air, fire, and water. (The fifth element is spirit, which can represent itself.) Choose something that feels both aligned with the element it represents as well as the uniquely ethereal qualities of the unicorn realm. For earth, you might choose a limpid, sparkling crystal such as a celestite, apophyllite, moonstone, or spirit quartz. For air, you might choose a white feather, a silver or gold incense burner with cinnamon or vanilla incense, or a tiny bell or chime. For fire, you might choose a small white candle anointed with a thin layer of olive oil and rolled in glitter or a rainbow-tinted ceramic oil burner containing a tealight and a bit of lavender, cinnamon, or peppermint essential oil (floated on water, as is customary with essential oil burners). For water, you might choose an iridescent or spiraling seashell or a bit of colored beach glass.

There's no rush; take your time in assembling these items. After all, the process is part of the magic. With each item, wait until you find something that awakens a sense of wonder within you.

Usually, these items can go on your unicorn altar. But for the purpose of working your magic, you'll create a sacred circle of around four to five feet in diameter by placing each item at one of the four cardinal points surrounding you: earth at the north, air at the east, fire at the south, and water at the west. (To find these directions, you can use a compass or the compass feature on your phone.) You can do this indoors or out, wherever it feels most powerful and right for you to perform your magical work.

Once you have your elemental representations and you've chosen your magical spot, you're ready to enter the realm of enchantment.

The Realm of Enchantment

In truth, only magic is real. It's all enchantment all the time. But in this life experience, and particularly this culture (and the accompanying paradigm) in which we find ourselves, we must make an effort to deviate from the illusion of the mundane. In other words, we must consciously enter the magical realm, where we know the truth: that we are Infinity and Infinity is us, and that, as such, we can craft our world according to our desires. The more we do this, the more magic we bring into our everyday experience and the more magic we bring into the world.

The following exercise will initiate you into the realm of enchantment, make your magical power more accessible, and activate your ability to create positive change in alignment with your will. And even if you've done magical workings before, it will attune your magic to the bright, loving, pure, and potent vibration that is the unique territory and signature of the unicorn.

But *caveat magus* (magician beware): do not do this exercise unless you've read the entire book up to this point, satisfactorily completed unicorn portal keys one through five, and followed up with three to six of the "living and breathing" activities at the end of each chapter. If you have completed these steps, you're good to go. Such preparation will reliably purify you, steady you, and ready you for the successful execution of this practice.

Before performing this practice, I suggest bathing and dressing in clean white or light-colored clothing.

UNICORN PORTAL KEY #6:

Stand in Your Power

This key depicts a five-pointed star surrounded by a circle, a symbol of nature and magical power. It is a key of initiation into your magical work.

Once you've chosen where you'd like to work your magic, bathed, dressed, and placed your four elemental symbols around yourself at the cardinal points (see page 131), you're ready to begin. Note that if any of your elemental symbols features a candle, tealight, or incense, you will also want to have a lighter or matches handy.

Stand in the center of your circle, facing east. Stand with your spine straight in a comfortable, natural way and with your knees slightly bent. Close your eyes and take some deep, conscious breaths to steady your body, ground your energy, and clear your mind. If your air symbol is incense, light it. Then connect with the element of air by calling to mind things like wind in trees, small tinkling chimes, birds flying, and wind blowing on your skin and through your hair. Say:

> *Element of air, I call on you! Infuse me*
> *with inspiration, fresh energy, and healing*
> *power. Remind me that I am free.*

Feel, sense, and know that the spirits of air have arrived in your circle to witness and assist with your magical work. Say:

> *Element of air, you are here. Welcome.*

Turn now to the south. If your fire symbol features a candle, light it. Then connect with the element of fire by calling to mind things like the sound and warmth of a crackling bonfire, the fiery phoenix rising from the ashes, and the blindingly bright midday sun. Say:

> *Element of fire, I call on you! Enliven me with*
> *expansive joy, radiance, and positive action.*
> *Remind me that I am passionate and alive.*

Feel, sense, and know that the spirits of fire have arrived in your circle to witness and assist with your magical work. Say:

> *Element of fire, you are here. Welcome.*

Turn to face the west. Connect with the element of water by calling to mind things like ocean waves, mermaids, a bubbling brook, and a cascading waterfall scattering rainbows through the mist. Say:

> *Element of water, I call on you! Flood me with cleansing,*
> *fluent communication and harmonious flow. Remind*
> *me that I am pure and that my magic runs deep.*

Feel, sense, and know that the spirits of water have arrived in your circle to witness and assist with your magical work. Say:

> *Element of water, you are here. Welcome.*

Turn to face the north. Connect with the element of earth by calling to mind things like the soil after it rains, the silence of a cave, an ancient and deeply rooted forest, and a fertile field or green expanse of meadow beneath your bare feet. Say:

> *Element of earth, I call on you! Nourish me*
> *with grounding, comfort, sustenance, and the*
> *calm clarity of silence. Remind me that I*
> *am safe and beloved by Mother Earth.*

Feel, sense, and know that the spirits of earth have arrived in your circle to witness and assist with your magical work. Say:

> *Element of earth, you are here. Welcome.*

Face east again. Imagine that you are sending tree roots of light down from your tailbone, legs, and feet deep into Mother Earth. In your mind's eye, see and sense these roots traveling naturally deeper and deeper until they reach Mother Earth's molten core. See this core as a sphere of bright, golden light like a subterranean sun. Let your roots enter this sphere and drink up this light. See and sense it traveling up toward your body naturally, like electricity naturally moves from a plug to an appliance. When it reaches your body, sense it filling every body part and every cell, anchoring you into the grounding, energizing, balancing energy of the planet.

Now, from the crown of your head, send a trunk and branches of light up into the sky. See your trunk and branches grow and reach higher and higher until they exit the earth's atmosphere and enter a realm of pure diamond-white light: the color of stars. Plug your branches into this light and drink it down toward your body, sensing it move naturally—again, like electricity through a cord—down toward the crown of your head. Then see and sense it entering the crown of your head and moving throughout your entire body and aura, mixing with the golden light from the core of the earth. Feel yourself connecting with infinity and the realm of pure potentiality. Say:

Element of spirit, I call on you. You are here. Welcome.
As above, so below. As the galaxy is a spiral of light, so
magic spirals around me and within me. My circle is cast.
I am between the worlds: the place where magic happens.
[Name of solar unicorn guide], I call on you.

Inwardly see or sense your solar unicorn guide's presence at your right. Say:

[Name of lunar unicorn guide], I call on you.

Inwardly see or sense your lunar unicorn guide's presence at your left. Say:

[Name of each unicorn guide],
you are here, and I thank you.

*I now initiate myself to the practice of unicorn magic
and announce my intention to responsibly wield my
magical power. I know that I am one with All That
Is and that, as such, I have access to vast magical and
spiritual power. I claim that power now and choose to
use it for my own highest and truest good, and for the
highest and truest good of all. I devote myself to all that
is noble and true. I commit to continually releasing all
fear and stepping, again and again, into the courage to
do what is needed to create positive change in alignment
with the unique gifts and talents I have to offer the
world. I commit to living a life of lightness, laughter,
freedom, and joy while also doing everything I can to
bring waves of healing and grace to the world. I know
in my heart and fully trust that my most joyful life
experience is one and the same with living in the way that
will most benefit my fellow earthlings and the planet.
I give thanks for this opportunity, from this day
forward, to shine my light and wield my magic
with integrity, purpose, compassion, and love.*

Place your hands on your heart and feel immense gratitude for the magic within you and around you, and for all
the support you have in both visible and invisible realms.

Then open your palms as if you are directing this gratitude outward like an endless fountain of light. Say:

Element of air, I thank you.

Keeping your hands in this gesture near your heart, turn to the north. Say:

Element of earth, I thank you.

Turn to the west. Say:

Element of water, I thank you.

Turn to the south. Say:

Element of fire, I thank you.

Turn to the east again. Move your arms down so they are at a slight angle from your body and direct your palms toward the earth. Then reach your arms up in a V and direct your palms toward the sky. Say:

Element of spirit, I thank you.

Drop your arms and look to your right. Say:

[Name of solar unicorn guide],
I thank you.

Look to your left. Say:

> *[Name of lunar unicorn guide], I thank you.*
> *Thank you, God/Goddess/All That Is.*
> *Thank you, thank you, thank you.*
> *Blessed be. And so it is.*

You have now completed the ritual. You have called a lot of extra energy into your field, so you will want to ground yourself a bit to get back to normal. To do this, lie flat on your back and see or sense any extra energy in your aura draining downward into the earth like wet laundry dripping excess water into the soil. Know that a normal, healthy, balanced supply of personal energy will remain in your field and only that which is extra will drip downward back into the earth. After that, further ground your energy by eating something with carbohydrates such as toast, a bagel, oatmeal, a muffin, or a granola bar. If you prefer not to eat grains, cooked root vegetables such as carrots, parsnips, or potatoes are also viable options.

When we open to the unicorn, our lives will be permeated by the awesome power of nature. But the unicorn is part of the realm of enchantment as well. When we embrace one, we also embrace the other. They are inseparable.

Ted Andrews in
TREASURES OF THE UNICORN

Welcome, Initiate

You have now imbibed a healthy dose of that wondrous supernatural elixir we call magic, so do not be surprised if you feel a little intoxicated for a day or so—and even possibly slightly hung over after that. As you will come to know, it's all part and parcel of practicing magic and dwelling ever more frequently in the unicorn realm and the realm of enchantment.

Colors will be more dazzling, light will be clearer, and everyday encounters with flowers, birds, and butterflies will be filled with even more meaning and presence. Additionally, your intuition may be stronger, you may have vivid and powerful dreams, and you may feel guided to make changes in your life, which could be tiny, gigantic, or anywhere in between.

To make the most of this time of increased magic and positive transformation, be sure to drink lots of water, get lots of sleep, eat clean, steer clear of toxic people and environments, and generally take sterling care of yourself in every possible way and on every possible level. Keeping up with your daily meditation practice and working with your journal to record any strong intuitions you receive will also be of the essence.

Now that you have been initiated as a magical practitioner aligned with the realm of the unicorn, you might be wondering: So what? And what is magic for, exactly? And how does it work?

Magical Dynamics

As one who has heard and answered the call of the unicorn, magic is intrinsic to your identity and your spiritual path. As such, the more you work your magic, the more you will feel like yourself. Not only that, but you will be doing a priceless service to magic—and unicorns—in general: you will be increasing the overall magic quotient in the world. You will be reminding other people of their magic and of the joy in cultivating wonder, bringing purity to mind, body, and spirit, and being a devotee of beauty. Consciousness is like electricity: when directed properly, it can light up whole towns, cities, and nations, and send messages instantly across the entire world.

On the personal level, you can create positive change according to your will. Of course, you already do this when you want a cup of tea and then make yourself a cup of tea. You affected the physical world in such a way that you brought forth a desire from your conceptual mind and placed it squarely and solidly into your hands. And in a way, that is already magic. But a conscious magical practice intensifies and magnifies this ability so that you can bring forth rent money or a summer romance or wild success at a job interview without having to know the physical process it will go through in order to materialize. With magic, you simply know that it will, indeed, materialize. You feel it, you sense it, you trust it, and then you magnetize it into your life experience.

In the movies, magic brings things in a flash or a puff of smoke. Your manifestations likely will not be as flashy or as instant as that. Rather, they will be more natural. (Remember how super-duper natural magic is?) You'll do the money spell, and the minute you stop watching and waiting for the money to arrive, you will receive an unexpected windfall or be presented with a lucrative opportunity. You'll do the romance spell, then you'll sort of forget about it, and then you'll crave strawberries at a random time and meet the love of your life in the produce aisle of your local grocery store.

Why magic works is a mystery that likely will never be solved. How it works—while still mysterious—is something of another story. Just by doing magic, you will learn the way it often plays out because you will witness it working firsthand. Still, for instructive purposes, here's a rough overview of the practical dynamics of magic:

You enter into magical consciousness. In this chapter's portal key initiation ritual, you did this systematically when you called on each of the elements in turn. This reminded you that you are one with All That Is and brought a sense of balance and equilibrium to your interconnection with the natural powers that be.

You state your intention, inwardly or aloud, and feel it to be already manifested and true. By stating what you choose to manifest and then feeling as if it's already manifested, you dial in the vibration of what you are choosing. Because the entire universe is pure energy and vibration, this sets in motion a magnetic action so that your vibration attracts its match.

You release your intention. Let's say you want to send a note to a friend who is across the room, so you fold it into a paper airplane, draw back your hand, and prepare to launch it. As you know, the note will certainly not reach its target if you don't let go of it at the end of your arm's trajectory. Similarly, if you set your intention and feel it to be true, and then don't relax and consciously release attachment to that intention, it will be impossible for it to go out into the ether and bring forth what you desire.

You joyfully and lightly look forward to the manifestation of your intention. Releasing attachment means not obsessing or worrying, but rather happily expecting your intention to manifest in the best and most magical possible way. It also means letting go of how it manifests or when it arrives or what exactly it looks like, and letting it take its natural course. It's very similar to the way the hungriest people in a dinner party always receive their meals last: they are so attached to eating and so overwhelmed with the vibration of hunger that it throws up a block to the vibration of satiation, which causes something of a delay. (Arguably, this is the most challenging part of working magic, but don't worry, you'll get the hang of it. Furthermore, it'll get easier and more natural over time as you learn to trust that your desires will, indeed, manifest.)

Your intention manifests in a 100 percent natural and possibly unexpected way. Often, magical success looks like something that might have happened all on its own anyway. And it is! At all times there are countless probabilities and possibilities. Working magic simply makes one of them more probable and possible than the rest.

The unicorns were the most recognizable magic the fairies possessed, and they sent them to those worlds where belief in the magic was in danger of failing altogether. After all, there has to be some belief in the magic—however small—for any world to survive.

Terry Brooks in
THE BLACK UNICORN

Living and Breathing
MAGIC

To integrate all that you just read and to actualize it in your life experience, choose to perform at least three of the exercises below. For extra credit, do all six or do one of them more than once.

1   Make a magical playlist. Just like magic, music is vibration. Now that you're initiated into your magical power, find songs that empower you with the vibration and strong inner knowing that you are magical. Listen to them often.

2   Choose what you will manifest. In your journal, assess and document the qualities and conditions you'd like to use your newly activated power to magically manifest. State each one in the present tense, as if it's already true. To make sure you remember the various areas of your life, use these headings: Spirituality and Self-Improvement, Career and Life Path, Friendship and Travel, Creativity and Playfulness, Love and Romance, Radiance and Recognition, Wealth and Prosperity, Health and Family, and Feeling at Home in the World.

3 Receive magical guidance from your unicorn guides. Through visualization and intention, spend time in meditation making contact with one or both of your unicorn guides. See what they show you, teach you, or give you to fuel your power and help you along your magical path.

4 Gift yourself with an initiation talisman. The initiation ritual in this chapter was intense. Congratulate yourself and signify your spiritual advancement by buying or making a pendant or other magical adornment (cloak, bracelet, tattoo, crystal, etc.) that feels like an appropriate symbol of your magic.

5 Conjure up a unicorn sighting. For fun and to exercise your magical chops, as soon as you wake up in the morning, joyfully and playfully expect to see a unicorn. Conjure up the ecstatic feeling of seeing a unicorn and bring the reality vibrationally into your field. Then, all day, playfully look for it and continue to expect it. (Remember to look everywhere. You could see your unicorn on a bumper sticker, an Instagram post, or a scene in a movie.)

6 Cleanse and rearrange your altar. After this chapter, you have new altar items! Also, you're a magical practitioner now. So take everything off your altar, give it a good dust or wipe down, and artfully arrange everything according to what feels exactly right. Maybe even add some fresh flowers or an apple as an offering.

The unicorn holds many secrets: the
secrets of jungles and moonlight; the
secrets which lie hidden at the roots
of trees and conceal themselves in
coral labyrinths beneath the ocean.

Josephine Bradley in
IN PURSUIT OF THE UNICORN

seven

NATURAL POWER

The fairy realm is the conscious presence and aliveness of the natural world. Wherever green and growing things thrive without human encroachment, wherever bright sunlight and fresh air create sparkles on pristine, natural bodies of water, and wherever birds and butterflies frolic, fairies are there. But they are not just figurative: they are unique beings with distinct thoughts, feelings, and behaviors, just like you and me. In fact, more than one person I know has caught fairies in photo and video, appearing in broad daylight in the form of glowing points of pink or green light, hovering near trees or flying through the air in playful swirling patterns like otherworldly fireflies.

Unicorns, too, are fairies: they are among the most rare, magical, and sophisticated denizens of the fairy realm.

As we have seen in previous chapters, unicorns are both alchemists and magical allies. In this chapter we will explore their special affinities for particular aspects of the natural world, including crystals, herbs, flowers, trees, and animals. You'll also learn how to work with these natural materials and beings in order to enhance and amplify your spiritual practice and magical work.

Crystal Consciousness

Like unicorns, crystals are of the earth and also transcend the earthly plane to align us with the realm of the Divine. Each gem and mineral possesses a distinct wisdom and vibration that can anchor and enhance specific energies in order to support you in your spiritual journey and magical work.

In this section we'll look at some of the crystals uniquely aligned with unicorn energy and particularly relevant to those of us drawn to the magic and wonder of the unicorn realm.

But first, here are a few general guidelines and practices to keep in mind.

You don't need a million crystals. While it's not impossible that you will genuinely feel guided to amass a considerable collection of crystals, this isn't the least bit necessary. An unspoken cultural value in the West is "more is better"—e.g., more shoes, bigger houses, and all the latest gadgets. But this isn't a valuable value; it's a value that has been artificially imposed by those who have a vested interest in perpetuating it (i.e., people who sell things). I want to draw attention to this because crystals often can be an area where spirituality spills into materialism. Don't let this happen to you; just one crystal is plenty. (As you will see, it's recommended that you obtain one for the unicorn portal exercise below.) More than one is fine, of course, but practicing a minimalist philosophy when it comes to crystals can help keep their magic pure and potent for you. After all, living light in all life areas helps you to keep the current of divine wisdom and spiritual sustenance wide open and flowing.

Only choose crystals that sing to you. When you go crystal shopping, you will likely encounter many, many beautiful gemstones, but only occasionally will one of them sing to you. For some, a singing crystal means you will actually feel it vibrate in your hand. For others, it means simply gazing at it will spark a feeling of love in your heart, and you will not be able to imagine leaving the store without it. For still others, when you hold it, you will feel a sense of expansion, energy, joy, and aliveness, or possibly a deep current of serenity, stillness, and calm. There also will be days when you will enjoy many crystals, but none of them will sing—but don't despair. While that will mean no new crystal, it will also mean all your money stays in your wallet.

You don't need to keep your crystals forever. Crystals are not actually yours. You don't own them. They own themselves, and they belong to Mother Earth. Most of them will outlive you by centuries. Your path has simply intersected with their path for a time, so don't hoard them! While some may stay with you for quite a while, be sure to honor their sovereignty by passing them on to someone else, releasing them back to the earth, or placing them in a natural body of water as your intuition dictates.

Cleanse and activate your crystals regularly. One of the reasons crystals like to work with humans is because we can cleanse them in order to activate their spiritual wisdom and magical properties. In many ways, this brings them to life and gives them an outlet for active participation in the evolution of planetary consciousness.

To cleanse and activate your crystal for the first time, first run it under cold water or place it in a moving body of clean water for at least three minutes. (One exception would be salt-based crystals such as selenite and Himalayan pink salt crystals, as these will slowly dissolve in water.) Then place it on a white cloth in bright sunlight for at least five minutes. Finally, smudge it with the smoke from a bundle of dried white sage for a minute or two. (Do this safely, making sure to hold the sage over a dish or plate to catch burning embers and to extinguish it fully.)

In the future (unless you feel intuitively guided to repeat the above process), you can choose just one of the three cleansing/activating methods: running water, bright sunlight, or white sage.

Empower your crystal with an intention and keep it with you. To employ your crystal for spiritual and magical use, choose an intention that is aligned with its magical and metaphysical properties. It can enhance the specificity and potency of your intention to phrase it in the form of an affirmation—in other words, a positive statement phrased in the present tense, as if it is already true. For example, if you're working with a crystal to increase your self-esteem and inherent sense of worthiness, you might choose the intention "I am beautiful, lovable, and worthy of every wonderful thing." If you're working with a crystal to relieve stress and promote serenity, you might choose the intention "I am safe. I am calm. All is well."

Once you've chosen your intention and affirmation, hold the crystal in your right hand and direct the energy of your intention into it as you clearly and confidently state your affirmation. Do this at least once daily while actively employing the crystal for this purpose, then keep the crystal with you throughout your day.

As promised, here are some crystals that are particularly aligned with the unicorn realm.

AMETHYST is a violet-hued quartz with a deeply soothing and spiritual vibration. It helps relieve stress, calm the mind, heal addictions and addictive behaviors, and promote restful sleep. It's aligned with the crown chakra and brings healing by reminding you of your oneness with the Divine.

ANGEL AURA is a clear quartz treated at a high temperature with platinum and silver, resulting in a beautifully iridescent appearance and uniquely whimsical vibration. This stone enhances creativity and helps activate the ability to channel spiritual wisdom from the angelic, fairy, and unicorn realms. Its uplifting and inspiring nature helps alleviate depression, lethargy, and fatigue.

APOPHYLLITE is a starlight-colored, luminous, bright, clear white stone that often appears in small pyramid-like shapes. When used in tandem with meditation and visualization, it can help you enter into other worlds and dimensions, including the fairy, unicorn, astral, and angelic realms.

AQUA AURA is a clear quartz treated at a high temperature with gold, resulting in a surprisingly bright aqua or bluish-teal hue. This stone is a powerful ally for periods of transition, particularly when you are concerned with differentiating yourself from your family and culture of origin by finding your own voice and making your own way in the world. It can help you know your truth so that you can speak it, act on it, and live it.

AQUAMARINE is a pale blue stone reminiscent of the clearest tropical oceans and most pristine alpine streams. It's highly purifying to the body, mind, and spirit, and can help relieve any sense of uncleanliness or toxicity. As such, it's great to use in tandem with a regimen of spiritual or physical cleansing. Additionally, it can help remove harshness in communication, heal the effects of criticism or insults, and open the flow of loving speech spoken or written.

KUNZITE looks very much like pale pink ice. It has a softening effect on the heart and emotions, and it can open the heart to love. This makes it useful in healing any sort of relationship issues, including challenges with family, friends, neighbors, coworkers, business partners, and romantic relationships.

LARIMAR is an opaque, vibrantly colored stone that looks like a slightly more aqua-toned version of the brightest blue sky after it's been purified by heavy rain or strong wind. Simply glimpsing a larimar can infuse one with a sense of deep and abiding joy. Indeed, it's a crystal that can help bring back our joy when it seems to be lost. Larimar can help us remember to prioritize joy every single day.

LEPIDOLITE is a sparkly lavender-colored stone that is perhaps the answer to this question: If a unicorn were a crystal, what would it be? Like a unicorn, it reminds us to love freely and with the purest of hearts. It also reminds us that we are lovable, beautiful, and deserving of endless blessings and miracles. Carrying it or wearing it can help attract true, deep, and lasting friendship and love.

MOONSTONE may resonate particularly strongly with your lunar unicorn guide. A pale milky white or yellowish stone, it holds the ethereal, receptive, dreamlike energy of the moon. It helps us turn up the volume on our intuition, remember and gain wisdom from our dreams, and harmonize with the moon's waxing and waning cycles of power and magic.

PERIDOT, a pale grass-green crystal, holds the serene and comforting vibration of a late summer day. Working with it can help you harmonize with the magic and wisdom of herbs, flowers, trees, and the harvest cycle of the seasons. It can also help strengthen your physical and mental health, facilitate healthy habits, and enhance feelings of grounding, inspiration, and interconnection with all life on earth.

SPIRIT QUARTZ is a quartz covered with many smaller crystal points that are called drusy, resulting in a beautifully sparkling effect. It appears in clear, amethyst, aqua aura, and angel aura varieties, and in addition to their individual properties, all of these can help foster a harmonious sense of community and interconnection. Additionally, spirit quartz boosts energy, creativity, inspiration, wonder, vitality, and joy.

SUNSTONE, as an energetic counterpart to moonstone, will likely resonate with your solar unicorn guide. With its radiant, peachy, golden iridescence, it contains the warming wisdom of our solar system's center and crowning jewel, the sun. Like spending time outside on a mild, sun-drenched day, working with sunstone can help facilitate authentic feelings of love for yourself and all of life, as well as gentle and consistent feelings of happiness, pleasure, joy, and contentment.

If you want to find the secrets of the universe, think in terms of energy, frequency, and vibration.

Nikola Tesla,
PIONEERING ENGINEER,
INVENTOR, AND PHYSICIST

Beautiful Botanicals

All green and growing things have an affinity for the unicorn, just as the unicorn has an affinity for the entire natural world. Still, certain flowers and herbs stand out as allies and associates of the unicorn and botanical residents of the unicorn's domain.

Furthermore, as a practitioner of unicorn magic, you may sometimes find it desirable to work botanical magic or simply be aware of the unique power and wisdom of the plants that indicate unicorns are likely to be near. As such, before we examine unicorn-resonant botanicals, here are some general guidelines for magically mingling with these powerful plants.

When you encounter these plants in nature, you will know that unicorns may be near. You might like to take a moment to gaze at the plant and honor its innate magic, power, and wisdom. You could even enter into meditation and quiet contemplation with it as you receive its wisdom in the form of a vibrational infusion and healing adjustment to your personal energy field. Additionally, offering a libation of blessed water, ale, or champagne can be a beautiful way to express your love and devotion to both the herb and the unicorn realm to which it belongs.

When you grow these plants in your garden or yard, you will simultaneously be strengthening your bond and vibrational alignment with the unicorn realm and your unicorn guides. As such, care for them lovingly and with great reverence. (Guidelines in the surrounding paragraphs will also be relevant.)

When you obtain parts of these plants specifically for magical use, do so with love and awareness. If you are purchasing them from a store, do your best to find organic, non-GMO herbal or floral suppliers. Then empower the herb or blossom in bright sunlight, and infuse it with your intention before use. If you are gathering them from nature or your garden, be sure to do so gently and with gratitude, and to offer something in return, such as a blessed libation (see above), a crystal, or a shiny silver coin such as a clean quarter or dime. Any of these can be placed near the base of the plant.

While you will find a collection of spells and rituals in the back of the book, here are some general methods of botanical magic that draw upon the five elements.

To work botanical magic with the earth element, place one or more of the herbs and flowers outlined below in a glass bowl. Hold the bowl in sunlight and empower the herbs with your intention, then lovingly bury them at the base of a unicorn-aligned tree. For a list of unicorn-aligned trees, see the arboreal alchemy section later in this chapter.

To work botanical magic with the air element, on a windy day, place one or more of the herbs and flowers (for our purposes here, dried is best) outlined below in a glass bowl. Hold the bowl in both hands and empower the herbs with your intention. Then climb to an elevated place and release the herbs to the wind.

To work botanical magic with the fire element, safely build a bonfire or a fire in your fireplace. Place one or more of the herbs and flowers outlined below in a small basket made exclusively of wood materials. Hold the basket in both hands and empower it (and the herbs within it) with your intention, then throw the entire basket in the fire. (Please only do this if it is 100 percent safe. Don't take any chances with fire magic.)

To work botanical magic with the water element, place one or more of the herbs and flowers outlined below in a glass. Hold the glass in moonlight and empower the herbs with your intention, then find a clean, natural, moving body of water and pour out the herbs on its surface.

To work botanical magic with the spirit element, find or create an incense or essential oil blend employing one or more of the herbs and flowers below. Lovingly call on your unicorn guides and clearly state your desire or intention. Then burn the incense or diffuse the oil as an offering and intentional act.

The following herbs and flowers are uniquely resonant with the unicorn realm:

APPLE is perhaps the botanical most aligned with unicorns. Magically, it can help bestow and enhance sweetness, beauty, love, friendship, and health. In addition to being aligned with unicorns, it's sacred to love goddesses such as Venus, Freya, and Aphrodite. While the entire tree is a unicorn ally (see the arboreal alchemy section below), you can also employ the fruit, seeds, and blossoms in your magical work. Apples and apple blossoms are excellent offerings for your unicorn guides and the entire unicorn realm. The seeds can be employed in spells, rituals, and charms.

CENTAURY, an otherworldly, lavender-hued bloom, is a wonderful ally for unicorn people as it helps us to channel our natural desire to love and serve while simultaneously taking care of ourselves and establishing strong, healthy boundaries. In addition to being an indicator of nearby unicorn presence (as all these botanicals are), centaury can help us be completely devoted to beauty and our spiritual path while also making time for self-care and saying no to requests and responsibilities that don't resonate with our true path or purpose. This can be helpful if it's easy for you to feel like a doormat, if you feel uncomfortably sensitive to the needs of others, and if you feel you're at the mercy of everyone else's needs rather than your own. To receive these benefits, spend time with centaury, employ it in your magical work, or take the flower essence (available at most health food stores and online) under your tongue or in water every day until you feel you've sufficiently absorbed its vibrational wisdom.

Please note that flower essences are not the same as essential oils. Flower essences are homeopathic remedies that contain the vibration of the flower rather than any part of the actual flower itself. Essential oils are almost the opposite: they are the concentrated therapeutic constituents of a flower or plant and are almost never taken internally.

CHICORY, especially when blooming, is irresistible to the unicorn and deeply in harmony with its essence. Discovering it in nature is a sign that you have entered the unicorn's domain. The homeopathic flower essence remedy is widely available in health food stores and can be taken to dispel excessive worry about your family, as well as the tendency to control or micromanage others. If you feel you could use help with these qualities, taking the flower essence regularly (until the qualities have cleared) will have the added benefit of removing blocks to owning your magical power, activating your intuition, and opening up to the unicorn realm.

CINNAMON has a high, sweet, pure, and strengthening vibration, much like unicorns themselves. Indeed, in Asia unicorns sometimes reportedly appear in tandem with the distinctive scent of cinnamon. The incense is a wonderful choice for your unicorn altar and as an aromatic accompaniment to any of your magical work. Ground cinnamon and cinnamon sticks can be employed in your rituals and spells. (Cinnamon essential oil is also available, but it is highly irritating to the skin, so be careful.) Empower powdered cinnamon and add it to your food to align more powerfully with the unicorn realm. Similarly, cinnamon can be imbibed in the form of tea.

CLOVER, while undeniably powerful, possesses a humble and unassuming stature. This mirrors its magical property of gentle power, which reminds us that one need not be forceful or imposing in order to quietly possess great mastery and wield immense authority. Remind you of anyone? That's right: unicorns. While they can be the gentlest of the gentle, they can also be fierce, and their power is vast. To absorb this essence, spend time with blossoming clover or employ the blossoms or famous triple leaves in your magical work. Red clover blossom tea and herbal extract can be taken internally for both healing the body and opening up to the unicorn realm.

FERN is an incredibly ancient family of plants. Spending time consciously gazing at a fern can sensitize you to the primordial wisdom of the earth beneath your feet. Fern's lush, otherworldly properties, as well as the miraculous fact that they are still alive and thriving today after existing for over a hundred million years on earth, are reminders of the pristine and untouched forest realm that is the unicorn's natural habitat. Magically, fern helps align us with our natural power while protecting us from harshness, toxins, and anyone harboring ill will. Lovingly gather a small bit of any variety of fern if you'd like to employ it in your magical work.

JASMINE, among the sweetest and most sensual of flowers, brings us into our body and senses, balances our sexuality, and helps heal old sexual wounds. It also helps attract love and romance. Work magic with jasmine incense, jasmine absolute (jasmine's natural fragrance oil), or the fresh flowers themselves. Green tea with jasmine flowers is also available, and—when infused with intention—makes for a wonderfully vitalizing and sensualizing potion.

LILAC is the unicorn incarnated as a flower. Have you ever noticed how rare and precious it feels to glimpse a lilac in any shade of its spectrums (white, pink, and purple)? While all flowers are fleeting, lilacs are among the most fleeting: they bloom in all their heady, mysterious splendor for mere weeks out of the year. And, like unicorns themselves, lilacs are aligned with the liminal and luminous—the space between the worlds of form and spirit—as well as intuition, gentleness, interconnection, and vast magical power. A blossoming lilac is, in fact, a portal: simply spending conscious time gazing at it and appreciating it will activate your intuition, remind you of your eternal nature (your true identity as a divine being), and transport your consciousness to the realm of magic, rainbows, and (of course) unicorns.

MINT—especially peppermint and spearmint—possesses a vibration unique in the intensity of its tingly freshness. Unicorns love its purifying and invigorating effects. Its magical benefits also include prosperity, vitality, clarity, and joy. Before working your unicorn magic or entering into any sort of unicorn-aligned spiritual practice, you might like to bathe in water to which you have added fresh mint leaves or a few drops of mint essential oil. This will dissolve heaviness and stuck energy while attuning your vibration to the realm of the unicorn. You can also employ the leaves or essential oil in your magical work or drink mint tea to internalize its essence.

MOSS, lush and thriving in a serene natural setting, is a strong indication that unicorns might live nearby. Magically, moss brings luck in all our endeavors. To employ it in your magical work, gently gather a pinch or two.

WATER LILY, like the unicorn, is aligned with both the moon and the sun. Indeed, the blossoms possess a cool brightness like the sun's radiance steadily emanating from the moon. Spending time gazing at a blossoming water lily confers the important quality of receptivity, which allows us to receive the many blessings the universe constantly wishes to bestow upon us. And, just as they are rooted in the dark, slimy muck at the bottom of a pond and reach up to the cleanest and most sun-drenched of blooms, water lilies can help us transmute all challenges and negativity into powerful blessings and love.

UNICORN PORTAL KEY #7:
Find and Consecrate Your Unicorn Crystal

Now, let us combine the fairy wisdom of crystals and botanicals to create your first physical unicorn portal key: your unicorn crystal.

This key will look precisely like the crystal you choose, and for the first time, you will be able to hold this key in your hand. It will open you up to the unicorn realm (like all the keys) and will additionally serve as a battery of spiritual energy and a wand for directing this energy in your magical work.

Visit a crystal shop (online if there are none in reasonable proximity to you) and, consulting the list of unicorn crystals above, find one that sings to you. It's ideal if this crystal appears in a single or double terminated point or has been purposely shaped to resemble a wand, as this will make it more ideal for directing energy. If necessary, take your time finding this crystal. You don't have to buy something on your first trip out. Wait until you know it's the one.

Once you've obtained it, cleanse it and activate it as described earlier in the chapter.

Next, consult the list of unicorn-aligned botanicals above. Choose one or two of them that feel right to you for infusing your crystal with vibrations that will be uniquely suited to you and your magical work. Depending on the botanicals you choose and what is available in your area at this time of year, obtain the corresponding incense, essential oil or absolute, or a tiny bit of the actual fresh or dried blossom or herb.

In front of your unicorn altar or out in a serene natural place, center your mind and breathe consciously. When you feel ready, infuse your crystal with the vibrational essence of the herb by bathing it in incense smoke, anointing it with the essential oil, or by placing the actual blossom or herb on a small dish or plate and nestling the crystal on top.

Imagine your crystal glowing and pulsating with iridescent, sparkling light. As you do so, say:

> *I now bless this crystal and consecrate it as*
> *a sacred ally and treasured magical tool.*
> *I give thanks to the Divine Spirit and Great*
> *Holy Mystery for this powerful relic, and I vow*
> *to use it with integrity, devotion, and love.*
> *Thank you, thank you, thank you.*
> *Blessed be. And so it is.*

The key is now yours. Place it on your altar until you're ready to employ it in your magical or spiritual work. (There will be examples of how to do this in future chapters as well as in some of the spells and rituals at the end of the book.)

In the future, you can refresh and recharge its magic by repeating the botanical infusion process (i.e., the incense bath, anointment, or by placing it on top of the actual flowers or herbs).

Arboreal Alchemy

As the fae creature who rules over the forest realm, the unicorn is naturally aligned with trees. Trees, in turn, have been considered potent symbols and anchors of spirituality in perhaps every culture on earth. Rooted deep in the power and nourishment of Mother Earth, and reaching up toward the glowing radiance of the cosmos and heavenly realm, they perfectly portray the practice and path of the healer, sorcerer, and spiritual warrior.

And, like crystals, flowers, and herbs, there are certain trees that are alchemically aligned with the unique magic and wisdom of unicorns. These can be found below.

Encountering any of these trees in nature will indicate the proximity of unicorn magic. You can plant them in your yard or seek them out for meditation, quiet contemplation, or to work magic under their boughs. In some cases you can magically interact with them in additional ways. When applicable, these will be included with the individual descriptions below.

SUGAR MAPLE reminds us of our roles as devotees of beauty. In Japan it's popular to practice *momijigari*, which is the conscious contemplation and enjoyment of the beauty of reddened maple leaves in fall. Additional unicorn values shared by the maple include wonder, creativity, and playfulness. Maple syrup, as a natural product of the tree, can be added to potions, beverages, and magical baths. A wand made of sugar maple wood would be a good choice for magic or energy work.

HOLLY is a fairy tree. Bringing a holly branch into your home near the winter solstice can help align your space with the realm of the fae (including, of course, unicorns). It's been held sacred by many cultural groups, including the Druids, the Romans, and some inhabitants of the Brazilian rainforest. Magically, it's protective, uplifting to the spirit, and energizing to the body, and it can be employed in charms and rituals to help manifest victory and success. The homeopathic flower essence remedy is widely available at health food stores and can be taken to mitigate feelings of jealousy and spite.

CEDAR is an ancient ally of pure positivity and light. Spending time with a cedar—or even simply inhaling the essential oil or incense—can help strengthen and enhance all the unicorn-aligned values within us: purity, beauty, intuition, healing, wonder, alchemy, magic, etc. In your magical and spiritual work, you can employ cedar twigs, wood, greenery, incense, and essential oil to break spells, clear negativity, create sacred space, clarify and focus your thoughts, inspire wisdom, and bolster the potency of your energy field.

APPLE is the tree most associated with the Isle of Avalon (of the Arthurian legends) as well as the vision of the afterlife (held by some magical traditions) known as the Summerlands. With such impressive credentials, it should come as no surprise that it's also been said to be the arboreal equivalent of the unicorn itself. Work magic with apples, apple blossoms, and the apple tree for youthfulness, beauty, feminine power, self-love, self-approval, romantic love, and to remember that life is sweet and blessings want to flow into your life experience. Simply blessing an apple with any one of these properties and then eating it can be a wonderful way to internalize this tree's magical power.

Animal Allies

Unicorns treasure all life and have deep respect for the well-being of every creature, from the diminutive gnat to the colossal blue whale. Still, there are certain animals with whom the unicorn enjoys a particular affinity. If you happen upon one of them in nature, stop and observe. Watch closely. Listen deeply. Admire the animal's splendor and enchantment. Chances are good the animal will bestow an intuitive message, a blessing, or an infusion of wisdom; be awake to it and receive it with gratitude.

You may also encounter a messenger animal in another way, such as by hearing about it or encountering its image repeatedly. If you have three such instances with the same animal in a relatively short period of time (i.e., of encountering the actual animal, seeing the animal's image, or hearing about the animal), this is certainly a mystical communication from the realm of unicorns and the fae. In such a case, first ask yourself: If I had to wager a guess about the message this animal is sending me, what would it be? Even if you feel like you're making it up, make your best guess anyway. After that, check out the descriptions of the animal's totem wisdom below for added insight into the wisdom the universe is asking you to receive.

If you'd like, you can employ imagery or materials related to one or more of these animals in your rituals, spells, and on your altar. For example, if you discover a naturally shed bluebird feather, it could be a powerful addition to a charm for happiness and luck. You might add a peacock feather to your unicorn altar while you are magically supporting your (or someone else's) healing process. Or, if you want to bring about beautiful transformation in your life, you might burn a stick of incense and, with intention, draw or color a butterfly.

Additionally, you might like to attract some of these magical creatures to your yard; for instance, with a hummingbird feeder or traditional bird feeder, or with flowers that attract pollinators.

BLUEBIRD is a harbinger of happiness, love, joy, and peace. She is a bit of the pure blue sky in feathered form. She reminds us that no matter how stormy things have been, the sky will clear and your pleasure in life will be renewed. Indeed, simply seeing a bluebird is a sign that positive change is in the air for you: expect windfalls of prosperity, auspicious encounters, and lucky breaks.

BLUE JAY is a trickster and road-opener. He can help get your energy moving when you've been stuck, and he can refresh your outlook when you feel as if life has become stale. Blue jay reminds you to stand up for yourself: to set boundaries, speak your truth, and defend your territory.

BUTTERFLY, as we explored in chapter 2, is a master alchemist. She literally transforms herself from an earth-bound crawler to one of the most colorful and spectacular winged beings on earth. Butterflies remind us of the transcendence and immortality of the soul, as well as our ability to transmute challenges into blessings and pain into beauty. Be aware that while butterflies are insects, it's also true that all butterflies are fairies. Never doubt that when you spot a butterfly, the realm of the fairies is near.

DEER are among the unicorn's closest relatives. Both deer and unicorns appear whimsical and delicate at first glance, but both also can be fiercely protective when necessary. Male bucks and female deer are both incredibly sensitive to their environments as a result of the caution they need in order to survive hunters and other predators. On the other hand, deer will not hesitate to attack to protect their fawns, and bucks have been known to be aggressive at times, particularly during mating season. Honor a deer sighting as you would a unicorn sighting: with respect, wonder, and awe. Symbolically, deer's blessings include sensitivity, intuition, magic, beauty, and renewal.

DRAGON, like the unicorn, is the ruler of one of the four realms in Eastern cosmology. While the unicorn rules the forests, the dragon rules the deep and natural waters of the world. In Western symbolism the dragon is more commonly associated with fire. Both fiery and watery dragons are allied with unicorns. Fire dragons get us in touch with our passion and our power. Water dragons take us deep into our magic, dreams, intuition, visions, and the mysterious unknown. Dragons of both varieties can be petitioned and respectfully summoned for powerful physical and spiritual protection.

DRAGONFLY is the dragon's earthly ambassador, as he easily flies between our everyday human realm and the mystical realm of the fae. While he is certainly an insect, make no mistake: he is also a dragon. His messages and gifts include creativity, whimsy, wonder, playfulness, intensity, passion, and vast magical power.

HUMMINGBIRD moves his wings so rapidly that they become almost invisible to the human eye. This is reminiscent of the way the human and fairy realms coexist in the same space: each vibrates at a different frequency, making one (mostly) invisible to the other. Hummingbird is a tiny little creature, but the speed of his wings and metabolism indicate the shocking intensity of his energetic vibration. He is like a little fireball of magical power! His qualities and specialties include creativity, vitality, romance, and joy.

LION has been traditionally considered the unicorn's enemy. However, mythology changes with the times, and nowadays this rivalry is, in effect, extinct. In our present age, the unicorn loves and respects the lion, who is more strongly associated with majesty, strength, sovereignty, and the sun than perhaps any other animal. In turn, the lion has great esteem for the unicorn, who the lion considers his most luminous and reliable ally. While they may have different eating habits and life philosophies, thankfully, both grew weary of their division. It's a most auspicious and revolutionary shift: the two strongest and most radiant creatures are now working together for the victory of all that is good, beautiful, and pure.

PEACOCK, like the unicorn, is an uncommonly divine and otherworldly creature. Unlike the unicorn, he can't bear to hide himself away from most other creatures. He absolutely must be seen, admired, and adored. That's why he's an excellent ally when it's our intention to begin proudly shining our light and sharing our unique and magical gifts with the world. Additionally, peacocks possess some of the unicorn's powerful curative medicine, which is why naturally shed peacock feathers make wonderful healing talismans and charms.

PHOENIX, as we discussed in chapter 2, shares the unicorn's gifts of transformation and transmutation. This mythical firebird, like the unicorn (as well as the dragon and tortoise), is another one of the four guardians of the realms in Eastern mythology. While the unicorn presides over the forests, phoenix presides over the deserts and dry land. Consider working with phoenix in the inner realms—through things like imagery, ritual, creativity, and meditation—when deep healing, purification, and transformation are required.

ROBIN heralds springtime, happiness, and the dawning of beautiful new conditions. He's also a reminder to speak up about what's important to you, and to speak clearly, honestly, and with integrity.

SPARROW reminds us of the beauty in simplicity. Her wisdom was succinctly expressed in the Tao Te Ching: "When you are content to be simply yourself and don't compare or compete, everybody will respect you."[4] A sparrow sighting will ask you to imagine looking back at your life from your deathbed. Then sparrow will say, "Will you be more likely to regret not having more money and success, or will you be more likely to regret the times you forgot to enjoy all the simple blessings that constantly surrounded you, such as the mellifluous laugh of a loved one, the sound of wind in trees, and the fragrant steam rising from a cup of tea? These little moments, after all, are the very stuff of life. Unless you remember to pay attention, even now, life is passing you by."

SWAN is indeed a dear friend and close ally of the unicorn, sharing many of the unicorn's wise and magical qualities, including purity, transformation, beauty, intuition, sensitivity, and romantic love.

TURTLE/TORTOISE rules over the swamps in Eastern mythology, just as unicorn rules over the forests, dragon rules over the waters, and phoenix rules over the deserts. A creature of infinite patience and mindfulness, turtle/tortoise reminds us of Mother Earth's steady blessings of

---

4   Stephen Mitchell, *The Tao Te Ching: A New English Version* (New York, Harper Perennial, 1988), 8.

grounding, nourishment, and healing. Few creatures are as wise as he. Listen deeply to his silent knowing and you will learn many things ... or perhaps just the one thing that you most dearly need to know.

The more I experienced herb magic the more I realized its true powers. It may well be the most ancient and yet the most practical form of magic, for its tools grow all around us...

Scott Cunningham in
CUNNINGHAM'S ENCYCLOPEDIA
OF MAGICAL HERBS

Living and Breathing
NATURAL POWER

To integrate all that you just read and to actualize it in your life experience, choose to perform at least three of the exercises below. For extra credit, do all six or do one of them more than once.

1 Take a slow walk in a forest. Notice the plants and animals that surround you. Appreciate their beauty and listen deeply to their wisdom. Feel that you are bathing in the magical energy that surrounds you. Stop along the way, as you feel guided, to spend time with a tree, chat with a bird, or gaze at a flower. If you'd like, sit down with your journal and jot down anything that feels important when you get home.

2 Go to a botanical garden. See how many unicorn botanicals you can find, and also attune to the sacred and magical frequencies of the other flowers, plants, and trees. Learn their names. Gaze at them deeply. Smell them. Appreciate them on a deeper level than you ever have before, as living fairy creatures of great power and enchantment.

3 Hang a bird feeder. Place it somewhere that allows you to comfortably and frequently watch the birds. If you choose a hummingbird feeder, be aware that it needs to be taken apart, washed, and refilled at least every other day. Traditional feeders are much less labor intensive, only needing to be washed every two weeks or so (but probably refilled a bit more often than that).

4 Plant a unicorn botanical in your garden or yard. If any of the trees or plants listed above would do well in your area, and you'd like to care for it, plant one in your yard. This will invite unicorn energy into your home and life. Every time you care for it and spend time with it, you will increase your vibratory alignment with the unicorn realm.

5 Create art that depicts one or more of the unicorn's animal allies. Let it be a magical act by setting an intention before you do so. For example, if you'd like to increase your magical power, you could set the intention that "I am a powerful magical being." (It's always best to phrase intentions in the present tense, as if already true.) Then you could draw, paint, sculpt, or even color (if you find the right coloring book) a fire dragon.

6 Try some elemental herb magic. Revisit the elemental magic instructions in the Beautiful Botanicals section above. Choose an intention, herb, and element, then work your magic by following the directions provided.

*Though magnificent beasts, they
are also wild animals, and wild
animals are dangerous.*

Nick Alverson in
LET'S STOP PRETENDING UNICORNS
AREN'T DANGEROUS

eight

COURAGE

Yes, unicorns are sweetness and light, but they are not all sweetness and light. They are also mystery and shadow, idealism and action, and even fierceness, aggression, and righteous anger. They will go out of their way to avoid stepping on insects and allow tiny birds to braid their shining manes with feathers and moss, but they will also not hesitate to fight to the death to protect themselves, their home, and those they care about. They stay hidden from the human world not out of shyness or fear, but out of a fundamental disagreement with many of the values that are exhibited by our mainstream culture. In fact, unicorns are social creatures and are well loved by their many friends in the forest and natural world.

You, dear unicorn ally, would do well to heed their example. While it's wonderful to allow your sensitivity and compassion full rein, without the simultaneous courage to be who you are, step outside your comfort zone, and take action on your dreams and the causes you care about, your life will seem boring, static, and stale. You will lose the passion and wonder that called you to this path in the first place. Your body may even begin to cry out by showing you signs of illness and lethargy. And your soul's light will slowly dim, depriving the world of the unique healing and magic only you can offer.

Of course, by its very nature, moving out of our comfort zone is always uncomfortable. Speaking up and speaking our truth can be terrifying at times. Taking action on our dreams, desires, and the causes we care about can activate our vulnerability and even sometimes our feelings of resistance and shame. But, as the unicorn teaches us, being courageous in daily life is also exhilarating, enriching, and necessary. It's necessary for our own well-being and also for the well-being of the world.

If we fear one thing above all, it should be to let fear hold us back from living the lives of our dreams.

Your Wildness

It's easier to live your courage when you also own your wildness. What is your wildness? It's the largest part of your DNA and your ancient evolutionary roots. It's the part of you that sees an open field and wants to run through it, that feels laughter flow through the deepest part of you like wind through an aspen grove, and that never hesitates to frolic in the sparkling ocean waves.

Of course, it's also the part of us that wants to push someone when we get angry, chew our food with our mouths open, and stomp our feet when we don't get what we want. (Clearly, there are reasons our elders saw fit to domesticate us.)

Now, though, you are at a point in your personal evolution when you can respect the manners you have learned while still wielding your wildness with mastery. You can learn to feel its current pulsating through you like a djembe drum, but you need not act on every single impulse it suggests.

Can you feel it there, beneath the language and the manners and the sophistication? Breathe in deeply. Breathe out fully. Repeat. Let your breathing follow a natural rhythm, but pay attention to when you are breathing in and when you are breathing out. After this paragraph, stop reading for a moment, and continue this attentive breathing until you begin to feel yourself inhabit a deeper part of your body and soul. Continue even longer until you tap into the vastness at the heart of who you are. All the emotions are there: all the love, all the anger, all the courage, all the fear. All the laughter is there too, and so is the desire to push people and chew sloppily and run wildly through the waves. It all simply awaits your presence and patience as you breathe into it all and let it be what it is.

This vastness is where your true courage lies, as well as your deep inner knowing of who you are and why you have come here into this human form. Your passion, your anger, and your love are arrows pointing to your path.

The mastery comes from reconnecting to your true, eternal, wild nature and then, moment by moment, choosing which impulses are appropriate to let rip and which are not. (Yes, stand up for yourself. No, don't punch anyone. Yes, now's an appropriate time to ask that person out on a date. No, it's not an appropriate time to lick their face.) Do be aware that reclaiming your wildness will cause you to be conscious of more everyday pain in the form of vulnerability, passion, and heartbreak. But it will also cause you more everyday joy in the form of elation, power, and true success. So you see, masterful wildness is the only viable choice. (Unless you long for a life filled with numb mediocrity, which I know you don't.) Besides, we can even learn to love the pain and let it be a portal to even more beauty. Poets do it all the time.

Owning Our Heartbreak

If the most popular #unicorn posts on Instagram are any indication, today's mainstream unicorn associations most often involve cupcakes, children's birthday parties, and blow-up pool toys. But the unicorn's more traditional roots involve many a sad story of being hunted, killed, and cruelly exploited. And what else would you expect? Perhaps more than any other symbol, unicorns broadcast the message of purity, integrity, and the pristine magical power of the untouched natural world. Considering the increasingly harmful behavior of humans toward each other and the planet in recent centuries, one can see why our predecessors told stories of this pure-hearted creature being slaughtered, ensnared, and betrayed.

Heartbreakingly, one also can see why today's unicorn symbolism is often so two-dimensional and plastic. While we may still enjoy the symbol, many of us have given up on the ideal of preserving the pure heart and soul of nature and have relegated it to the realm of child's play— something appropriate for sparkly stickers and whimsical cake decorations, but nothing more. Additionally, some of us have become so disheartened by what we see happening to our planet and in the world, we prefer to retreat into our sparkly rainbow world of candy and plush toys.

This is not to discourage you from occasionally enjoying unicorn-themed birthday treats and other colorful or shimmery merchandise. Rather, it's to acknowledge that those of us drawn to unicorn wisdom are not two-dimensional or shallow or childish, and it will not serve us to believe that we are. We are, in fact, deeply alarmed and pained by the institutionalized suffering of other people, animals, plants, air, water, and the entire planet.

In addition to acknowledging this painful truth, the entire world will benefit when we also choose to own it, feel it deeply, and transmute it into beauty through creative action and artistic expression.

What's more, once we own the emotional pain we carry (from all sources), we become empowered to heal it. Doing so allows us to move forward in every area of our lives without being hampered by fear. Owning our pain shows us that even if we encounter something that hurts, we can do more than just handle it: we can heal it, transform it, and emerge stronger and wiser than we otherwise could have been.

UNICORN PORTAL KEY #8:

Own Your Deepest Pain

If you examine your memories of times when you were overtaken with grief or heartbreak or longing, you will discover that those feelings were rooted in love. Why else would your heart have been in so much pain? And when you look even deeper, you see that wherever there is love deep enough to cause you pain, there is also the most profound joy. Because love is what we are here for, and joy is the reward for feeling that love, even at the expense of our pain. That's why, for those of us who choose to own the darkest midnight of our pain, that pain eventually cracks our hearts open to the blinding sunrise of our joy.

This etheric key glows with the rosy radiance of dawn after a particularly long and dark night.

To obtain it, sit in front of your unicorn altar or somewhere else where you won't be disturbed. If you'd like, light a candle and some incense. Sit with your spine relatively straight in a comfortable way. Set a timer for twenty minutes, then close your eyes and breathe. Notice your breath and allow it to deepen. Continue to breathe while noticing when you breathe in and when you breathe out. When your mind wanders, even if it's been doing so for some time, as soon as you notice, simply bring your attention back to your breath. Once the timer dings, open your eyes.

While this is a simple practice, it is also profound. Bringing your attention back to your breath allows your breath to get into deep places in your body, mind, and spirit. If there is stagnant, unhealed, or festering emotional pain, it will touch on that pain and the pain will begin to move. That's why it's a good sign if you feel resistance or boredom: push through anyway and you will uncover the pain. It's also a good sign if you find yourself crying, whether or not you understand why.

Try this just once, and you'll know firsthand: it takes courage. If you made it twenty minutes, you were courageous indeed. (To reiterate, successful completion of the breathing portion of this exercise does not need to entail perfect attention to your breath. Minds wander; it's what they do. As long as you bring your mind back to the breath whenever you notice it wandering, you're fulfilling the requirements for this key.)

Now that you're in a receptive and open state, feel into your deepest heart. What pain is presently living there? Write it in your journal.

I am in pain because Mother Earth is being exploited. I am in pain because polar bears are losing their habitat. I am in pain because my parents got a divorce when I was three. I am in pain because I miss my cat since she died last year, and I wish I could

have done more to save her. I am in pain because I say mean
things to myself when I look in the mirror. I am in pain because
I'm worried I'll never be good enough. . .

Continue until you've been as honest with yourself as
you possibly can be and mentioned every emotional ache
and wound you can currently detect. If you can cry after
you've come to this point, that's wonderful. Crying is a
beautiful saltwater bath for your soul. If not, though,
don't force it.

Next, look at what you've written and feel the pain
as fully as you can. Get in touch with the deep ache in
the center of your heart. Then create art out of the ache:
paint, draw, sculpt, collage, create a short film, choreo-
graph a dance piece, or write a song, poem, play, or short
story. Even if you don't think of yourself as creative, create something for the sake of the exercise: you don't have
to show it to anyone if you don't want to. And don't hold
anything back out of politeness or care for others. Transforming pain into art can be a great blessing to the world.
For example, remember the times you've been struck by
the beauty of life and love while listening to a sad song
(like "Yesterday" by the Beatles or "Wild World" by Cat
Stevens) or watching a heartbreaking film (like *Moonlight* or
The Deer Hunter). Funny or sweet art can also be powered

by pain, such as the movies *Wall-E, Bambi,* and *Harold and Maude.*

Once you've created your art, you've earned the key. Congratulations! Close your eyes and imagine adding it to your collection.

Authenticity Over Safety

Now that you've chosen to feel your pain, how do you feel? Fine, right? And possibly, in a way, even better than you did before? As you can see, painful feelings are not the most crushing and damaging thing to your soul. Resisting and suppressing painful feelings, on the other hand, cryogenically freezes your joy.

This brings up an important point. For unicorn people like us, it's important to get the hang of telling the difference between our intuition and our fear. For example, most of us feel some natural shyness before going to a party where we don't know a ton of people. Usually, our reticence to get enthusiastic about the party is not our intuition telling us not to go. Rather, it's our comfort zone asking us to stay in it. The problem is, if we listen to our comfort zone, we'll never go anywhere fun or meet anyone cool. In these cases, we must push through the initial inertia and get ourselves out in the world. Quite often, once we do, we are rewarded with wonderful things such as exhilaration, fun, opportunities, and supportive new friends.

Of course, sometimes our intuition actually is telling us to stay home and not go to the party. For example, if you've been going full steam and you haven't taken any downtime for a while, your body and emotions might need some time to regenerate with a blanket and a good book. There might be something about the party's host (or any other aspect of the gathering) that doesn't feel totally right to you, and your intuition is giving you the tip-off that the party isn't actually somewhere you'll want to be. That's why it's important to tune in deeply and see: Is this just fear of moving out of my comfort zone or might it actually be my intuition alerting me that something isn't for me? This isn't just true for parties. It's also true for career decisions, creative projects, travel opportunities, personal relationships, and other situations.

Don't worry: if you're committed to being honest with yourself, you'll be able to tell the difference if you simply choose to look a little deeper into your feelings. Additionally, in the next chapter, you'll be cultivating a deeper and more vital relationship with your intuition.

Eleanor Roosevelt said, "You must do the thing you think you cannot do."[5] This points to an important clue: if there's something you deeply wish you could do, but you think you can't, that's your comfort zone asking you to stay in it and not your intuition at all. This, for instance, is why so many people are so acutely afraid of public speaking. It's a fear that has a bite to it because deep down, most of us actually adore the idea of standing in front of a crowd, saying words that are important to us, and then being heard, understood, and appreciated for what we have to say. You can notice this pattern, also, in those who go out of their way to assure everyone that they are terrible writers or artists or dancers. They are shutting down their joy for fear of being vulnerable. Of course, few of us are perfect at something the first time we try it, but being perfect isn't the point. Living our lives is the point: giving things a try when we think they might open us up to the flow of everyday adventure and ecstasy, whether or not we impress people or win any popularity awards.

With all of this in mind, make a list in your journal of the things you would like to do but think you cannot do. What ideas make your heart beat a little faster? What makes you feel uneasy or even terrified but also exhilarated

5   Eleanor Roosevelt, *You Learn By Living: Eleven Keys for a More Fulfilling Life* (Philadelphia, PA, Westminster Press, 1960), 30.

to contemplate doing? I'm not talking about legitimately dangerous things like standing in the middle of a busy freeway. I'm talking about life-enriching things like playing bass in a band, getting your PhD in child psychology, or moving to Asheville, North Carolina. Breathe deeply as you brainstorm, remembering what Fritz Perls (founder of Gestalt Therapy) famously declared: "Fear is excitement without the breath."[6] Consider a roller coaster and you will clearly see that the line between fear and excitement is the very definition of fun. And choosing to walk that line is what allows you to follow the example of the unicorn by living a courageous and joy-filled life.

The Valiant Heart

In this world we are often trained to do what is known as "playing it safe." This looks like a lot of different things, but it often involves putting a damper on your dreams in some way. For example, when you say you want to be a film director, your parents might tell you, "That's a hard life. It's a better idea to get a business degree and find a job with a good company." Or, when you say you want to move to New York City, your best friend may say (in a disapproving tone), "Wow! But you've never been there.

---

6   Gay Hendricks, *The Big Leap: Conquer Your Hidden Fear and Take Life to the Next Level* (New York, Harper Collins, 2009), 18.

You don't even know anyone there, do you? And it's really expensive, isn't it?" If we let them, even facial expressions and vocal inflections can discourage us from moving forward on our dreams.

Of course, your mother, father, best friend, or anyone else who may express discouragement is not usually doing so with malicious intent. Usually they are doing it for one or both of the following reasons: (A) because they are worried about us, and (B) because they are afraid of following their dreams and it makes them feel uneasy when someone else does.

It's important to separate the world's tendency to frighten us away from our dreams from what is authentically true for us personally. Is it hard to be a film director? Yes. It takes a lot of work. But when it's work you care about passionately, it's joyful work fueled with enthusiasm. You know what's much harder than working passionately with enthusiasm all day? Working at a job you don't care about, day in and day out. Perhaps you will get paid more reliably and consistently, but if your days are drab and uninspired, are you truly wealthy? Might it be more accurate to say that true wealth is getting to wake up and do what you care about all day? Similarly, if your heart truly desires to move to New York City, you must move there!

If you realize you don't love it or it's too expensive, you can always move back home or somewhere else altogether. But the only alternative to following your heart is living your entire life wondering what it would have been like if you'd followed your heart. Talk about expensive! That's much too high a price to pay.

So now that you've gotten clear on the things your heart of hearts is asking you to do, take action on them. Take one step toward a dream, and then another. Keep moving forward and pushing through the fear. That's what courage is. The root *cour* means "heart." Living with courage is equivalent to living with heart. Indeed, without courage, the radiant sparkle of your heart will slowly but surely diminish. You mustn't let it! Stoke that sparkle straight-away!

If you trade your authenticity for safety, you may experience the following: anxiety, depression, eating disorders, addiction, rage, blame, resentment, and inexplicable grief.

Brene Brown in
THE GIFTS OF IMPERFECTION

Living and Breathing
COURAGE

To integrate all that you just read and to actualize it in your life experience, choose to perform at least three of the exercises below. For extra credit, do all six or do one of them more than once.

1. Take a class in something by yourself. It's best if it intimidates you just a little. Consider kundalini yoga, ballroom dance, tarot, rock climbing, Spanish, or any other relatively safe thing that, when you think about it, fuels your inspiration but also slightly scares you. Don't invite any friends along! Friends are great, but for the purposes of this exercise, you must go by yourself.

2. Repeat the breathing meditation from the portal key exercise once daily for seven days. Twenty minutes of conscious breathing for seven days straight requires intense courage, and it will not fail to open you up to your wildness and activate powerfully positive change in your life. Will you accept the challenge? Remember: it's not about perfection. It's just about being as present as possible and bringing your attention back to

the breath whenever you notice it wandering, no matter how long it's been.

3 Choose one of your dreams, and for the next seven days, take one action step toward it. It doesn't need to be a big action step. For example, if it's your dream to get your degree in art therapy, simply researching colleges on the internet is one action step. On the second day, you could identify a few that really call to you. The third day, you could see what their entry requirements are. A fourth action step could be researching the cities in which the schools are located and seeing which ones seem the most intriguing to you. A fifth could be looking at housing options around the schools you're considering. A sixth could be researching financial aid. And a seventh could be taking a look at the application requirements for one of the schools.

4 Create another work of art out of your pain. If you feel so inspired, repeat the activity in the portal key exercise by creating one or more additional beautiful works inspired by your heart's deepest pain.

5 Identify a cause that inspires your sense of protectiveness, and take action on it. For example, if you feel like fiercely fighting for animal rights, volunteer at or contribute to an animal rights organization, or attend a protest or demonstration on behalf of animals.

6 Do the thing you think you cannot do. If you often find yourself telling people what a terrible artist you are, then create art. Do you wish you could write but are pretty sure you're just not that talented in that area? Write. Do you sometimes fantasize about dancing freely in public, but you're fairly certain you have no rhythm? Go out dancing.

*The sixth [brow] chakra is also
called the third eye . . . It relates to
the pineal gland, the light-sensitive
organ within the brain that is
responsible for visions, dreams, and
the cycles of sleep and waking.*

Anodea Judith in
CHAKRAS

nine

INTUITION

You are a genius of subtle energy and intuitive information. When you trust this to be the truth, you are plugged into an endless stream of loving, reliable guidance that inspires you, protects you, and tells you precisely what you need to know.

As you will recall from chapter 4, the third eye chakra is the area at your brow that is related to your psychic abilities and intuition. Additionally, as a human unicorn ally, you might say you have an invisible horn of light extending from this energy center: a spiraling, shimmering antennae that may be invisible to most naked eyes but is nevertheless present in the form of radiant energy. This horn can both broadcast and receive information, and it acts as a conduit that allows you to perceive messages from the Divine, other people, and the natural world.

In this chapter, you will become more sensitized to your intuitive gifts and discover how to employ them with increasing confidence and skill.

The Secrets of the Universe

Unicorns are incredibly subtle creatures. Their sensitivity is so immense, in fact, that it causes them to hide away in the most remote and untouched corners of the forests to shield them from the hard lines and harshness of the human world. At the same time, their sensitivity is what makes them such formidable allies: they are so aligned with the subtle currents of the cosmos, they can ally with the energetic momentum of the moment like the most masterful of ninjas and dexterously ride the energetic ocean like a surfer on the most colossal of waves.

You, too, have access to these precious powers. If you've read this far and you've been faithfully completing the recommended exercises, chances are good you're already starting to sense the more subtle reality and (whether or not you consciously realize it) you've likely begun to receive intuitive guidance in various forms.

While intuitive guidance and information about the subtle reality always comes to us in the form of energy and vibration, there are a number of ways you might perceive it.

You might see it. You may receive visual information in the form of light, color, words, or images in your mind's eye or with your actual eyes.

You might hear it. You may receive auditory information in the form of words, sounds, or music in your mind or with your physical ears.

You might smell it. You may receive olfactory information in the form of scents or strong memories of scents.

You might feel it. You may receive information from touching certain objects or you may feel physical sensations that alert you to intuitive information. Areas of your body such as your stomach or fingertips may become extra sensitive, tight, or tingly. Or, you might receive emotional information in the form of feelings.

You might know it. Finally, you may just know things without being told and without having any other tangible reason for knowing them.

If you're not already sure of the ways you receive intuitive information, here's a useful clue: it's likely you casually use language that indicates how you are intuitively oriented. For example, over the next few days, try noticing which of the following phrases (or ones like them) you most often use.

Visually oriented intuitives say things like "Here's how I see it..." "I see," and "See what I'm saying?"

Auditory intuitives say things like "I hear what you're saying" and "Sounds good to me."

Olfactory intuitives say things like "Something smells off" and "I'm sensing a change in the wind."

Sentient or feeling intuitives say things like "I feel you" and "I feel like..."

Cognizant intuitives say things like "I know what you mean" and "Wouldn't you know it?"

Of course, you may say something similar to all of these at various times, which would be an indication that you are a multisensory intuitive. It's certainly not uncommon to receive intuitive information in more ways than one.

Noticing the ways you receive intuitive information helps you to recognize it more frequently when you do. The more you recognize your intuitive guidance, the more you validate the information you're receiving and the stronger your intuitive current becomes.

Visions and Dreams

In addition to being open to receiving intuitive information through your feelings and senses, you will receive signs, visions, and dreams. You can then easily interpret these in order to align your life even more thoroughly with the resonance of the cosmos.

For example, have you ever noticed a certain number combination showing up again and again in your life (such as 11:11), or possibly a symbol, animal, or other theme (such as frogs)? The vehicles for such recurring signs are endless: license plates, billboards, podcasts, films, nature, and conversations, just to name a few. When this happens so much that you begin to notice, it's a sign from the universe.

Before you go Googling the symbolic meaning of what you're seeing over and over again, go straight to your own intuition by asking yourself what you think it means. If you answer (as you likely will) "I don't know," ask yourself again. But this time, add the phrase "if I had to guess." So, you'd say to yourself, "If I had to guess, what do I think it means?" This will bypass the part of you that has been trained to only know things when you have learned them from a source outside of yourself, and it will therefore allow you direct access to your clear and power-ful intuition.

After that, if you'd like, you can go ahead and look up the traditional symbolic associations with the sign you have been seeing. For example, 11:11 is often seen as a reminder that you are able to manifest the true desires of your heart, and frogs are symbols of wealth, abundance, and luck.

When they feel significant, dreams can be interpreted in an identical way. Ask yourself what you think your dream means. Then add the magic words: *if I had to guess*. Every time you employ this seemingly simple secret, you will surprise yourself by how accurate and helpful your dream interpretations will be.

Visions may arrive in the form of daydreams, or you may see certain images, pictures, or stories in your mind while you are doing something such as meditating, show-ering, walking, or driving. Sometimes their meaning will be obvious. Other times you may need to pull out the "if I had to guess" trick, which will not fail to yield helpful and accurate results.

UNICORN PORTAL KEY #9:

Activate Your Third Eye

This exercise is both fun and powerful at the same time. You will be consecrating and decorating the area at the center of your forehead: your third eye chakra, the seat of your intuition and the location of your invisible spiraling horn of light. This will help you recognize your identity as an intuitive being and remind you that it's in your nature to receive psychic information and divine guidance.

If you look with your inner vision, you'll see this key looks very much like a unicorn horn made of moonlight and rainbows.

You will need:

* lavender essential oil (if you have sensitive skin, you'll want to dilute it with a carrier oil, such as sunflower or sweet almond)
* one or more materials to decorate your forehead, such as henna, face glitter, temporary tattoos, sticky jewels, or a bindi (a bindi is an adhesive forehead ornament that is available online and at many Indian import stores)

First, you might want to light some candles and incense on your unicorn altar to set the mood. Next, relax and take some deep, conscious breaths. When you feel centered and calm, very lightly anoint the center of your forehead with the lavender oil. Say:

My inner light is sacred. My inner sight is strong.

Take some more deep breaths. Feel your mind clear and divine light enter your forehead as the oil absorbs into your skin.

When the oil has been absorbed (you can also wipe it off if you need to), begin to adorn your forehead in any way that feels right to you. Just a single bindi is great, but feel free to get as elaborate as you like. As you decorate, do so with the intention to honor your clear inner knowing and connection to the Divine.

When your decoration is complete, gaze lovingly in a mirror. Say:

I am a divine child, beloved by
the unicorns and the universe.
I honor my intuitive gifts as aspects of my divinity.
I give thanks for my clear, bright, and
powerful psychic abilities.

Take a bit more time to breathe, close your eyes, and envision receiving the spiraling, shimmering key.

Now you can do whatever feels right with your adornment: leave it on or take it off. Go out into the world or stay in. Meditate, create art, dance, or go for a walk in nature.

P.S. If you post a picture of yourself with your forehead art, please use the hashtag #UnicornMagic!

The Path of Your Destiny

What is in the cards? Luckily, there are plenty of beautiful card decks out there designed to assist us with our intuition. So get yourself one and find out!

Both oracle cards and tarot cards serve as excellent guideposts toward your own intuitive wisdom. While popular culture sometimes portrays intuitive card readings as potential harbingers of doom, this need not be the case for you. In fact, when you begin with the clear and confident inner knowing that the universe is on your side, all you will see in the cards is loving and supportive guidance, helping you make choices that feel authentic to you and that lead you down the path of your heart's deepest joy.

If you've never read cards before, you'll probably want to start with an oracle deck rather than a tarot deck. Oracle decks are much more accessible to the beginner. Some of my favorites are *The Wisdom of the Hidden Realms* and *The Wisdom of Avalon Oracle Cards* by Colette Baron-Reid, as well as my own *Magic of Flowers Oracle.* You can also find decks specifically created for unicorn lovers, such as *The Magical Unicorns Oracle Cards* by Doreen Virtue and *Oracle of the Unicorns* by Cordelia Francesca.

On the other hand, if you feel drawn to working with the tarot, there's no time like the present to begin learning. An especially magical deck (and one with plenty of unicorns) is *The Star Tarot* by Cathy McClelland. I also like *Witches Tarot* by Ellen Dugan and find it to be a wonderful choice for those who are still getting acquainted with tarot basics.

Whatever deck you choose—and do wait until you find one that sings to you, glows brighter than other decks, or fills your hands with tingles and warmth—for the clearest and most accurate readings, spiritually cleanse it and consecrate it before you use it. You can cleanse your deck by safely smudging each individual card, front and back, with the smoke from a stick of cinnamon incense (make sure to catch any burning embers on a plate or incense holder). Then bathe each card (again front and back) in bright sunlight for a moment. Finally, hold your deck in both hands. Close your eyes and take some deep breaths. Imagine sending roots of light from your tailbone deep into Mother Earth and connecting with her glowing golden core. Feel her radiant golden light moving up your roots and into your body and energy field. Then imagine sending a trunk of light up from the crown of your head, out of Earth's atmosphere, and sending branches into the liquid, diamond-white light of Infinity. Sense this light moving down your trunk and into your body and energy field. Imagine Earth light and Infinite light merging and mixing throughout your body and becoming especially radiant at your heart. Then send this light out from your heart, down your arms, into your hands, and then into the deck itself. Take a few moments to strongly see and sense the deck pulsating with golden-white light. Say:

> *I now recognize and activate the divine power within this deck. By aligning my personal energy with the energy of these cards, I create a powerful resonance that will result in accurate, insightful readings that are for my own highest and truest good, and the highest and truest good of all. Thank you, Mother Earth. Thank you, Father Cosmos. Thank you, thank you, thank you. Blessed be. And so it is.*

Your deck is now cleansed, consecrated, and activated. If you'd like, you can sew or find a beautiful oracle card bag for it (Etsy has lots of good ones). Some card readers also like to keep a clear quartz crystal point with their deck to keep its energy clear, resonant, and strong.

Most oracle decks come with a guidebook containing instructions for how to do a reading. But you'll find two of the most basic ways to read oracle cards below.

For both types of readings, consider your question and phrase it properly. It's best if you ask for guidance rather than for a definitive yes or no answer. For example, "What guidance will best support me in deciding whether or not to move to Santa Fe?" will yield better results than "Should I move to Santa Fe?" Similarly, "Please give me insight into my potential relationship with Jason" will open the door to much more helpful guidance than "Should I go out with Jason?"

Once you feel good about the question you've composed, hold the deck in both hands. Take some deep breaths, center your mind, and call on the Divine. Become aware that you are a part of All That Is. Take this time to remember, also, that you are a divine child with access to divine wisdom. When you feel ready, ask your question inwardly or aloud, then shuffle the deck in any way you like.

At some point, you'll get the sense that it's time to stop shuffling. Some people feel it in their hands, some people hear it in the sound of the cards, and some people just know. Be assured that there is no wrong way to receive the inner nudge to stop shuffling; whenever you stop will be perfect.

Once you stop shuffling, for a basic one-card reading, simply draw a card from anywhere in the deck. Take some time to look deeply at the image on the card and to get a feeling from what you see. See what intuitive messages you receive from simply looking at the image. How does it make you feel? What story does it seem to tell? Then look in the guidebook to see what the author of the deck says about the card you selected, and look deeply into its relevance to your question.

For a simple three-card reading, remove the top three cards from the deck and lay them faceup, left to right. The first card will represent the past, or the genesis of the issue. The second card will represent the present, or the core of the issue. The third card will represent the future, or the natural evolution of the issue. As described in the one-card reading instructions above, begin by taking some time simply looking at each image. Get a feeling for them. How do they make you feel? What stories do they seem to tell? What intuitive messages do they trigger for you? Then move on to reading the descriptions in the deck's guidebook. Take your time and look deeply into the ways this guidance may provide answers to your question.

If your first card deck happens to be a tarot deck (rather than an oracle deck), it's likely you have a lot more learning ahead of you before you begin to master your new intuitive tool. While tarot instruction is beyond the scope of this book, there are plenty of accessible resources out there to help you learn, including the website Biddy Tarot (biddytarot.com) and books such as *The Ultimate Guide to Tarot* by Liz Dean and *Tarot for Beginners* by Meg Hayertz.

Once you feel confident doing readings for yourself, if it feels right to you, you can also offer them as gifts to friends and family who might appreciate them.

Everyday Intuition

In truth, we are not separate beings; we are all connected, and we are all one. We are one with other people, animals, plants, the earth, and the entire universe. That's why intuition is not bizarre or exceptional; it's natural. Just as we can tell a lot by the nuances of someone's facial expression, we can also tell a lot by the energetic and vibrational cues we pick up in various situations and environments.

Once you accept that you have intuitive abilities and then choose to honor them, they will steadily become clearer, more accurate, and more powerful. Simply placing your attention on them will bring this about. It can also be helpful to have at least one supportive friend who honors their natural intuitive abilities as well. This way, you can share your discoveries, validate what you're experiencing, and even practice working with your intuitive gifts together.

Just like every intuitive person, there will be some things that come easily and naturally to you and other things that don't. Maybe you'll have deep insight into the emotions of those around you, but seeing future events isn't usually your thing. (Incidentally, the future is not singular or finite. So if you do see the future, you will likely see many possibilities.) Regardless of what you know or don't know, you can be honest with yourself and others about it. There's no reason to feel pressure to know something you don't or have access to information in a way that isn't in alignment with your inherent gifts.

Additionally, there are some things that can be helpful to relate and others that won't. This, also, is something to listen deeply to your intuition about. For example, let's say a friend who knows you are intuitive repeatedly requests information about her love life, asking things like "Is this guy trustworthy?" or "Should I move in with this person?" While in some cases, giving specific answers to such questions might be appropriate, when you tune into your intuition in this case, you may sense that giving her these answers isn't what is going to best support her. Instead, it will support her to encourage her to cultivate her own intuition about such things. In this case, you might ask her, "What do you think? Does he feel trustworthy to you?" and "Well, do you feel like moving in with him?" You may feel further guided to continue to ask questions after she answers these ones, such as "Why?" or "Why not?" or "What is stopping you from sharing these feelings directly with him?"

I share this because when we first get started on the intuitive path, we may sometimes feel pressure to "deliver" and to have it all figured out. At these times, we must remember that the point is not to impress people or to know more than they do, but to be a conduit of divine guidance and to relay it in the most loving and supportive possible way.

Similarly, when it comes to ourselves, it can be helpful to remember that we don't need to know everything or understand everything, nor should we expect to. However, we can trust that what we do need to know will be available to us precisely when we need to know it. Imagine, for example, that you are the one with romance questions, such as "Is this person trustworthy?" and "Should I move in with this person?" When you ask yourself these questions, you may not know the answers initially. And when you look deeper, you realize what you really need to know is that it's not time to move in with someone you aren't sure is trustworthy. Maybe in the future you will be more certain, but for now it's time to retain boundaries that feel authentic to you. So if you and this person were to discuss the possibility of moving in together, it would be important for you to clearly state that you're not yet ready for that step.

In both cases (whether it's you or your friend), you can see that the point is not to know all the answers. The point is to navigate this life experience with grace and authenticity, and to listen deeply to the current of divine wisdom that's available to you at all times. This way, you can fully immerse yourself in this precious, ultimately unfathomable life experience and continually deepen your wisdom along the way.

*Prayer is telephoning to God, and
intuition is God telephoning to you.*

Florence Scovel Shinn in
THE MAGIC PATH OF INTUITION

Living and Breathing INTUITION

To integrate all that you just read and to actualize it in your life experience, choose to perform at least three of the exercises below. For extra credit, do all six or do one of them more than once.

1. Be an intuition detective. For one full day, carry a notebook with you everywhere you go. Pay close attention to your inner senses and write down anything you receive. For example, do you see images with your mind's eye that give you information about a situation? Perhaps you hear words in your mind that help you make choices. Maybe your stomach alerts you when someone isn't being completely honest. And maybe you realize you "just know" something without knowing how you know. Be aware that these things may be related to anything in your life, from what college to attend to what brand of shampoo to buy. Also be aware that until you give them your full attention and respect, they may be the sort of things you would usually dismiss as "just my imagination" or "just a random thought."

2   Record your dreams. Keep a notebook or recorder by your bed and jot down or record any and all memories you have of your dreams. Later, see if you can interpret them using the "if I had to guess" technique described above.

3   Notice messages from the universe. Do you keep seeing or hearing about a number sequence, such as 12:34 or 444, or a particular aspect of the natural world, such as raccoons or palm trees? If so, what is the universe telling you? (Remember the "if I had to guess" technique.) Also notice if, for example, you're mulling over a particular question and a song instantly begins playing with lyrics that seem like the perfect answer. The universe is always talking to us, and things get wonderfully interesting when we choose to listen.

4   Get yourself an oracle deck. If you haven't already, take some time to find yourself an oracle deck you absolutely adore. Then cleanse and consecrate it and begin working with it. The best way to learn is to do!

5   Locate a friend who will talk to you about this stuff. If you already know just the friend, yay! Call them up, invite them over for tea, and get chatting! (You might even play around with your oracle cards if you have your deck already.) If you don't already know the friend, maybe put some feelers out with your existing friends to see if they might be awake to the realm of intuition and open to talking shop. If it seems like you might need to meet an entirely new friend, you might find them somewhere like a local tarot class (you can often find them at community college extensions or metaphysical bookstores), a yoga class, or a public magical gathering of some kind.

6   Write down a question you have, and then answer it. Phrase the question using the instructions in the oracle card section above. Then tap into your intuition to receive guidance. You can use an oracle deck or just relax, take some deep breaths, and look deeply. What do you sense? What feels right? Take your time as you find your intuitive way. Be sure to write down the guidance you receive.

Do whatever brings you to life,
then. Follow your own fascinations,
obsessions, and compulsions. Trust
them. Create whatever causes
a revolution in your heart.

Elizabeth Gilbert in
BIG MAGIC

ten

FREEDOM

Unicorns are paragons of freedom. Not only are they experts at staying free from traps of all varieties, they make it their mission to free any trapped being they may encounter, whether the trap is physical, mental, or emotional.

In fact, they are elusive for this very reason: their ability to move in and out of the physical form at will allows them to stay free from anyone who might wish to capture them. It also allows them to free wild animals from traps, birds from cages, and pets from unhappy homes. Additionally, they use their so-called "imaginary" status to flow in and out of the environments of children in harsh, abusive, and violent situations in order to bring them much-needed joy and sow the seeds of their future freedom.

You can learn from the stubborn freedom of these pure and regal animals to liberate yourself from limitations and traps of all varieties. You can also call on their energy and spiritual support in order to break old bonds, bust through old blocks, and establish glorious freedom in every area of your life.

Never Captured

Each time life presents you with a challenge or choice, your path takes a turn according to your actions and decisions. The unicorn reminds you that if you want to live the life of your dreams, you must do your best to avoid taking turns that will lead you into traps. Your activated intuition will help prevent this. It will allow you to look forward at each fork in the road and take the path that leads to a vision of you as wild, joyful, and free.

Be aware that your family and culture may try to trick you into taking a path that will end up as a trap: a huge student loan burden, for example, or a job you don't love or a house that ties you to a region where you'd rather not live.

Traps sometimes exist purely in our minds, but that doesn't mean they aren't traps. For example, thought patterns that tie us to a negative self-image are traps, as are habits of criticizing ourselves and expectations that we will fail.

Any time you find yourself saying, "My heart of hearts doesn't want to do this or to be in this situation, but I must" or "I really wish I could change this, but I can't," you are seemingly mired in something that isn't in authentic alignment with you. But you needn't be. You have the ability to free yourself. Maybe it will be challenging to free yourself from whatever seems to be currently trapping you. Maybe it will mean making a painful choice, maybe it will require meticulous discipline, or maybe it will take longer than you'd prefer. On the other hand, it could be something as simple and as instant as a shift in perspective. Regardless of the details, as an ally of the unicorn realm, it is absolutely in your power to be free.

Before we move on, grab your journal and make a list of every trap you seem to be in at this moment. Big, little, inner, or outer, write it down.

I feel trapped because I can't stop thinking negative thoughts about my body. I don't want to be in this school. I have to go to work even though I don't like it. I have to call my mom every week so she won't worry, but I wish I didn't have to.

Now, with each one, ask yourself: Do I *really* have to be in this trap? Inwardly investigate and see if you can find a possible way out, even if you're not ready to commit to it yet. For now, just look for possibilities. For example:

I could choose to stop thinking negative thoughts about my body and establish a new habit of loving the way I look. Maybe I can change schools or take a year off. Can I find a way to love going to work? If not, I could find a different job. Maybe I can talk to my mom about calling her less frequently. Even if that's not okay with her, it's my life; I can make the choice to call her once a month instead or send her a text instead of calling.

Next, make a decision for each one. You have two main choices: you can change the condition or situation, or you can leave it how it is. If you choose to leave it how it is, however, you will still be changing it by acknowledging that it's not actually a trap, it's a choice. In other words, if you choose it, it's not a cage. It's not beyond your control. As such, reframe the statement to say, "I am choosing to stay in this school." Then add why you are choosing it: "I'm choosing to stay in this school because it will create greater freedom for me in the future, in a way I want to be free." Or, "I am choosing to call my mom once a week. I am choosing to do so because I know I will feel better when I do."

Happy in Your Skin

Feeling secure on a deep level is a prerequisite to feeling truly free. When we have a sense that we are enough as we are and that it is safe to be in our skin, we are able to live in alignment with our dreams and boldly step in the direction of our desires. While you will, of course, still feel vulnerable at times (such as when you meet new people or try something that's outside your comfort zone), you will also have an abiding sense of self-love and a profound inner knowing that, at the deepest level, you are safe.

Lucky for us, if we ask, our unicorn friends will protect us with great integrity and devotion, and cocoon us in a warm sense that we are safe and all is well. If something is off in any situation or relationship (provided you remember to listen to your intuition), you can trust that one or more of your unicorn allies will alert you, while giving you the time and insight that will allow you to protect your sense of confidence and calm.

A unicorn is happy in his own skin, he loves himself and everyone around him. He chooses to live in the moment and doesn't dwell on the past (that's gone) or worry about the future (who knows what it will bring).

Sarah Ford in
BE A UNICORN & LIVE LIFE ON THE BRIGHT SIDE

UNICORN PORTAL KEY #10:

Shield Yourself in Light

This exercise will draw upon unicorn wisdom and magic to shield you in a protective bubble of iridescent light. This bubble will serve as an intuitive boundary that will help you know what you'd like to let in and what you'd like to keep out. It will also allow you to see the truth of love that is underlying almost every interaction and situation, rather than being stuck perceiving the surface layers of discord, harshness, or fear. This shield will protect your sensitive heart and nervous system from being bruised or battered by the thoughts and feelings of others.

As if all of that weren't enough, this shield will also ground you in the awareness that what others think of you is none of your business. This will remind you to focus on the joy of loving others rather than worrying about how much (or how little) others love you.

All of this will unlock your sense of true freedom.

This key is made of clear crystal, which subtly gleams with rainbow colors under the light.

Making sure you will not be disturbed, sit in front of your unicorn altar or out in nature. Close your eyes and breathe deeply and consciously. Continue breathing in this way until you feel extremely centered and relaxed.

Call on your solar and lunar unicorn guides. Ask them to completely clear away any and all stuck or challenging energies from your energy field. Request that they remove any unhealthy energetic cords of attachment between you and any person, condition, or habit. Continue to breathe deeply as you imagine them shining their solar and lunar light within and around you, cleaning up your energy field and releasing all undesirable connections. (You don't need to know what they all are, as you can completely trust your unicorn guides to heal what needs to be healed.)

Next, request that they completely fill and surround you in a bubble of light. Inwardly see and sense them bathing you in a perfect mixture of their golden-white solar light and silver-white lunar light, which combines to create a pure iridescent, crystalline light. Imagine every cell and molecule of your body being bathed and transformed in this radiance, and imagine it extending outward from your body to encompass you in a sphere of protective, shimmering light.

Decisively say or think:

> *Within this sphere, only love remains.*
> *Through this sphere, only love may enter.*

Now you may go out into the world with a sense of being safe and happy in your own skin, ensconced in a bubble of light and love. You can calmly speak your truth when necessary, and you can leave situations or relationships that aren't safe or that otherwise aren't in alignment with what's best for you.

Imagine receiving the key and slipping it onto your key ring.

Thank your unicorn guides, relax for a little bit longer, and open your eyes.

This sphere will remain potent for around twenty-four hours. I highly suggest refreshing it daily, perhaps first thing in the morning, last thing at night, or as a part of your daily meditation.

Dare to Set Boundaries

Unicorns and their allies are profoundly sensitive and loving beings. You must be sure, therefore, to keep yourself safe from guilt trips and other traps related to the egos or controlling natures of others. Even people who aren't expressly trying to control you can sometimes cause you to do something you don't actually want to do, such as volunteer or donate money when you don't authentically feel like it. Weak boundaries can even cause us to say yes to friends' invitations when we've been overworked and really just want to stay in and read a book.

One of the best ways for you to prevent your energy from being depleted is to remind yourself that everything is energy, and everything you send out comes back to you multiplied. From an energetic standpoint, for example, there is a big difference between donating money because you want to and donating money because you feel obligated to. The first is actual giving, to which the universe responds with giving back to you exponentially. The second is false giving. When you give falsely, you focus on the lack you feel and the guilt that pressured you into it. Since that's what you're sending out, the universe has no choice but to send it right back to you by increasing your lack and sending you plenty more reasons to feel guilty.

So what's a conscientious unicorn person to do? Each and every time someone makes a request of you or invites you to do something, tune into your natural feelings. Do you honestly want to do the thing or does it feel like something that will deplete you and take away from your sense of freedom, expansion, and joy? As challenging as it may seem at first, as you get in the habit of speaking your truth in these areas, it will become easier and easier over time.

What's more, behaving with meticulous authenticity in this way is not just beneficial for you, it's also beneficial to all concerned parties. To illustrate, imagine how you would feel if you knew a friend was just going out to lunch with you to "be nice" and didn't really want to go at all? Wouldn't you prefer that they stayed home so you could spend time with someone who was actually in the mood to go out to lunch? And when you're not contributing to causes you don't authentically want to contribute to, think of all the time, energy, money, and enthusiasm you'll have to contribute to the causes that make your heart sing, including your dreams and visions for your future and your chosen career path.

To gain clarity in these areas, grab your journal. Brainstorm a list of any and all areas in which you could have greater boundaries and authenticity. When, in the past, have you commonly responded out of guilt or obligation? Are there certain people around whom you feel controlled or like you can't fully be yourself? Are there certain situations in which you don't feel free? Write them all down, then spend time with each one. How can you shift your behavior with these people or situations to have clearer and stronger boundaries in the future? Write it all down and promise yourself you'll put time and effort into establishing these positive new habits of boundaries and personal freedom.

A Revolution in Your Heart

No one else is quite like you. In fact, no one else is even close. It's one of the most awe-inspiring things about this human experience to realize that we are all, each of us, completely unique and totally beautiful in our very own ways.

Similarly, no one else has your unique vision for what you want to do and what you want to create. You can tell someone "I'm going to open a restaurant" and they won't be able to glimpse precisely the restaurant you're seeing in your mind's eye, no matter how hard they try. Or you can say, "I want to paint murals on street corners" or "I want to travel for a full year before college" and no one will quite understand why your heart is burning to do exactly that or how it could possibly be a fabulous idea. In fact, some people—even ones who love you very much— may try to discourage you from acting on your creative impulses and unique personal desires.

But you're not alone. There are lots of people in the world who have led lots of amazing lives in which they did lots of amazing things, and not one of them was fully validated for their vision before they acted on it.

That's why an important aspect of being free is going your own direction and doing things your own way, despite the often well-meaning opinions of others. You are not betraying anyone when you do what your heart wants to do. But when you don't do what your heart wants to do, you are betraying yourself. And that's a trap.

True success, after all, is not something as trivial as making a million dollars or winning an Academy Award. While there is nothing wrong with such earthly validations—and you should definitely work toward them if that's what your heart of hearts desires—true success is simply living bravely and trying the things you want to try while you're here. Usually, if not always, true success includes plenty of "failure," which allows you to learn important stuff, like what not to do, how to do something better, or even that you actually want to take a whole other path entirely. In other words, success includes stepping forward into the unknown, stepping sideways, backward, up, down, and then forward again, and learning as you go. Ultimately, success is being who you are and living life with courage, whatever the path may bring. You know you're successful when you live a life you'll feel satisfied to look back on because you took the risks you wanted to take, whether or not your actions were "successful" in the eyes of the world.

Of course, this isn't everyone's definition of success. Choose a definition of success that resonates with your heart, and then live it!

An Illuminated Path

The word *freedom* is often associated with the idea of having no responsibilities, but this is not the kind of freedom the unicorn urges us toward. Rather, the unicorn desires for us the freedom that comes from working hard at something we're passionate about, day in and day out, with great discipline and focus. It's the freedom to forge our own way: to be beholden to no one but ourselves and to nothing but our own heart's desires. It's the freedom to know ourselves and, through the expression of our deepest truth, to set in motion great and towering waves of beauty that bless and harmonize everything in their wake.

Living this sort of freedom is not effortless, and yet the effort is not grueling, as it is fueled by passion and joy. At first, though, the effort required can feel insurmountable, as it often asks us to take steps that to others might seem insane, or at least odd, rebellious, or somewhat unhinged. For example, you might, like my significant other, Ted, work at a pizza parlor in a college town for almost a decade while you hone your musical craft, until one day your musical career takes off and everyone finally approves. Or you might, like me, read books about esoteric spirituality for years upon years, craft charms, spin spells, and talk to flowers while everyone you know wonders what the heck you are doing with your life.

While I can't guarantee you'll ever see the whole path, I can guarantee that you'll see the next step. It will be illuminated by what interests you: what sparks your sense of magic, wonder, and awe.

What I'm getting at here, dear and beloved reader, is be free. Live the life you want to live. Try what you want to try. Go where you want to go. Don't let anyone convince you to hide your light. Don't be tricked by any of the traps, and if you do fall into one, don't believe you have to stay in it. Take risks. Live your own definition of success. Take the step that is illuminated before you. And above all, be like the unicorn: be free.

In the infinity of life where I am,
all is perfect, whole, and complete.

Louise Hay in
YOU CAN HEAL YOUR LIFE

Living and Breathing
FREEDOM

To integrate all that you just read and to actualize it in your life experience, choose to perform at least three of the exercises below. For extra credit, do all six or do one of them more than once.

1 Free yourself from a trap. In the journal exercise in the Never Captured section in this chapter, choose at least one of the traps you identified and take steps to free yourself from it immediately.

2 Shield yourself in light for seven days straight. Repeat the portal exercise above once per day for seven days. After completing the initial seven-day challenge, I highly recommend that you continue with the habit, perhaps making it an integral part of your daily meditation.

3 Wear a reminder to honor your boundaries. At a craft store, find a piece of sparkly lavender or iridescent white yarn. Tie it around your left wrist as a reminder to take a deep breath and consult with your

authentic feelings before agreeing to anything or making any sort of commitment. Keep it on (replacing the yarn as necessary) until you've internalized the habit.

4   Do what causes a revolution in your heart. Don't wait for external validation before living your dream! Once you figure out what causes a revolution in your heart, take at least a single step toward it today. Tomorrow take another step, and the next day another, and so on.

5   Commit to the discipline that will help you live your freedom. Living the life of your dreams means being free, but that often entails working hard on a regular basis. What structure can you create that will help you live your freedom? If you're an artist, it might be creating art for ninety minutes five days a week, come rain or come shine. If your dream begins with moving to a new city, it might be saving the money necessary to make your move. Dream it, plan it, do it.

6 Do something you've never done but always wanted to do—especially something you haven't done for fear of what other people would think or how they would feel. Examples might include getting a tattoo, dancing on a street corner, or taking a road trip by yourself. Do it with the blissful awareness that you are free!

If you would be a magician, honor the Earth. Honor life. Love. Know that magic is the birthright of every human being, and wisely use it.

Scott Cunningham in
EARTH, AIR, FIRE, & WATER

eleven

Unicorn Spells

Dear unicorn devotee, in this final chapter you will find magical practices—formulas, recipes, charms, and incantations—specifically created for you, the unicorn-loving spiritual practitioner. Each is designed to help you bring about a specific condition in your life and in the world.

After all, as a unicorn ally and initiate, you have magical power to create positive change according to your will and intentions. You do this by aligning with the Divine—also known as the Infinite, the Great Mystery, and God/Goddess/All That Is—in order to shift energy in such a way that your experience of the physical world shifts as well.

If you think you've never done spells or rituals before, you're wrong! If you will recall, the portal key exercise in chapter 6 was actually a somewhat involved magical ritual. In fact, when you invoked the elements for that ritual, you were casting a magical circle. Before the rituals you'll find below, you might like to repeat the circle-casting process in order to create sacred space before working your magic. You can also just perform the rituals as they're written. Follow your intuition and create magic in a way that feels right to you.

The other portal key exercises were also forms of magical work, so you are actually quite a bit more experienced than you previously may have realized.

But in case you still feel like somewhat of a beginner, think of each magical endeavor you embark on as an experiment, and have fun with it. Remember that the most important ingredients (and ultimately the only ingredients you really need) are your clear intention and your conscious connection with All That Is. The rest is just really fun and sparkly window dressing. Or, more specifically, the ingredients and instructions are like focal points or anchors that help you to connect with the Infinite while setting your sights on your desired goal.

As you perform some of the rituals and spells outlined below, you'll begin to learn to follow your intuition, and in no time you'll be crafting your own practices to perfectly fit your preferences and goals. If you're wondering which one to start with, as you read, notice the practices that particularly appeal to you and that unmistakably fill you with blissful beauty and sparkly serenity. That's your intuition giving you a nudge.

Most of the practices in this chapter are optional and may or may not feel appropriate according to your current goals and situation. Still, there is one I highly suggest you perform at some point soon, and that's the final unicorn portal exercise. It is a celebration of all you've learned and your final initiation into the magical, majestic, mystical realm of the unicorn.

Spells for Happiness and Joy

Let's begin with one of our most fundamental desires as humans: the desire to feel joy. These rituals will help you find happiness and rediscover your harmonious nature.

SUNSHINE SPELL TO BREAK THROUGH THE GLOOM

This spell is perfect for dissolving a gloomy mood, reversing negative momentum, and generally opening the skylights to the sunshine of happiness and joy.

Ingredients
- ✳ a hand mirror
- ✳ a vase of daisies
- ✳ a white or sparkly white cloth

Perform this ritual somewhere pleasant outside, on the day of a new moon, when the sun is bright and shining. It can be in a yard, garden, park, or serene natural setting, provided you're certain you won't be disturbed.

Sit comfortably and relax in front of the mirror and flowers. Take some deep breaths and center your mind. Feel the solid earth beneath you and the vibrant sun on your face and shoulders. When you feel sufficiently grounded and present, call on your solar unicorn guide by saying,

> *[Name of solar unicorn guide],*
> *I call you to my side.*
> *Please dissolve the gloom and turn the tide.*
> *Inner sunshine grant to me*
> *So I am blissful, happy, and free.*

Breathe deeply as you feel the sunshine cleansing your body, mind, and spirit and disinfecting you of old, lingering shadows. After you feel sufficiently cleansed, hold the mirror up to the sun to absorb the energy of the sunlight.

(Be sure to aim it upward so it doesn't catch anything on fire.)

After just a minute or so, wrap the mirror in the cloth to contain the energy within it. Say:

[Name of solar unicorn guide],
I thank you deeply and well
For answering my call and fulfilling my spell.

Feel gratitude in your heart for a moment or two longer, then go home with all the ingredients in tow. Place the wrapped mirror and flowers on your unicorn altar. First thing each morning for the next moon cycle—and whenever you need an extra dose of sunshine—unveil the mirror and aim the reflective side at the center of your chest area. Feel yourself receiving a shot of brightness and joy directly into your heart. Then wrap it back up and place it back on your altar. Leave the daisies until they're past their prime, and then lovingly release them to the earth or a compost bin.

MOONLIGHT SPELL TO WAKE UP TO WONDER

Has life become ho-hum and humdrum? If so, this must absolutely change, as wonder—if you will recall from the first chapter—is the only truly appropriate response to this wonderfully wondrous life experience. This spell will help you reawaken your latent sense of wonder.

Ingredients
* ❋ ylang-ylang essential oil
* ❋ your unicorn crystal (see chapter 7)

On the night of a full moon, bathe and dress in something clean and white. When the moon is shining brightly in the sky, go outside to where you will be both safe and undisturbed. Stand in the moonlight. Take some deep breaths until you feel centered and calm. With your unicorn crystal in hand, open the bottle of ylang-ylang oil and take a whiff. Savor the scent as you feel yourself soaking in the moon's silvery rays. Call on your lunar unicorn guide by saying:

> *[Name of lunar unicorn guide], please be here now:*
> *Gallop with the moonlight's gentle glow.*

Feel your guide arrive. Feel blessed by its luminous presence. Say:

> *I thank you, sweet [name], for answering my call.*
> *Please awaken me now to the magic of all.*

Smell the ylang-ylang again, gaze at the beauty of your unicorn crystal, and continue to absorb the moon's rays. Feel that they are illuminating and enhancing your awareness of the magic of life, charging you up like a magical battery. Stay for as long as it feels right, and then thank your unicorn guide one last time from the bottom of your heart. The spell is complete.

RAINBOW CHARM TO FILL YOUR HOME WITH JOY

This fragrant and colorful charm will bless a home with wave upon wave of joyful energy. Make it for yourself or give it as a gift.

Ingredients

* 7 ribbons, one in every color of the rainbow, about ½ yard each in length
* 9 rosemary sprigs

First, empower all ingredients by placing them in bright sunlight for 1–2 minutes. Then tie the rosemary into a bunch with the ribbons, placing the ribbons end to end and tying them in a bow. Hold the charm in both open palms and visualize bright, beautiful rainbow energy filling and surrounding the home in a blinding blitz of color. Inwardly summon your connection with the unicorn realm to powerfully bless the space with love, light, laughter, and every wonderful thing. Feel gratitude and know that it is done.

The best place for the charm is on or above the front door, inside or out. You can refresh it regularly (perhaps every few months or so) by removing the ribbons, releasing the rosemary to the earth or a moving body of water, and repeating the process with nine fresh sprigs of rosemary.

Spells for Wealth and Prosperity

This is an abundant planet, and the universe wants to support you in every possible way. These spells can help you tap into the natural flow of prosperity that is your birthright.

FULL MOON CHARM FOR FINANCIAL INCREASE

This spell will supercharge your wealth. After performing it, you will notice an increase of financial opportunities and windfalls. For best results, work in tandem with the universe to stimulate your finances. In other words, be sure to act on any intuitive nudges you receive and to work hard if a lucrative prospect is presented to you.

Ingredients
* a moonstone that has been cleansed under cool running water and dried
* a scrap of kelly green fabric
* a small length of lavender or purple ribbon
* cinnamon essential oil

On the evening of a full moon, after moonrise, assemble all ingredients. You can do this indoors or out, as long as you won't be disturbed.

Call on your lunar unicorn guide by saying:

[Name of lunar unicorn guide], I call to you.
Please lend your magic bright and true.

Hold the moonstone in your open right palm. Say:

On this sweet and magic night,
I create this charm with full moon's light.
May wealth and increase now be mine,
As with abundance I align.

Imagine what it will feel like to have plenty of money flowing in: more than you expected, more than you dreamed of. Feel those feelings now. Dial them up and celebrate as if you are already experiencing this abundant financial flow. Feel gratitude.

Tie the moonstone into the fabric with the ribbon. Anoint it with a drop of the cinnamon oil. (Be careful not to get the oil on your skin, as it is a harsh irritant.) Say:

Like the moon whose light abounds,
My wealth shall grow in leaps and bounds.
With joy that my wealth shall grow and swell,
[Name of lunar unicorn guide], I thank you well.

Place the charm on your altar. Keep it there for at least three additional full moons, refreshing the cinnamon oil at each one.

WATERFALL SPELL TO ATTRACT A NEW INCOME STREAM

This is a powerful nature spell that will help you attract one or more new generous streams of income.

Ingredient

❋ a waterfall under which it is safe to stand

Near the waterfall, take some deep breaths and center yourself. When you feel relaxed, consciously draw upon your connection to the unicorns and the unicorn realm. Remember your portal keys and all your earnest efforts to tap into the unicorns' generous powerhouse of magic and mastery. Then set the clear and strong intention to draw one or more generous streams of income into your life and bank account. Feel the feelings that go along with this as if you have already fully manifested this goal into form. Step into the waterfall. Feel the water streaming around you like an unending flow of money and wealth, activating your prosperity and tuning your vibration to the frequency of abundance.

If you don't have easy access to a safe waterfall, you can also do this spell by safely wading in a stream, facing upstream, and letting the water rush around your calves.

CINNAMON SPELL TO
CONJURE UP SOME CASH

Money is just a form of energy. If you ever find you are in immediate need of a pile of the stuff, you can use your unicorn-aligned sorcery skills to call in that cash.

Ingredients
* a cinnamon stick
* an organic apple

Before sunrise, find your way to a unicorn botanical (tree, flower, or herb—see chapter 7) growing somewhere outside. The more unicorn-aligned the area (i.e., the more likely you perceive it to be the potential stomping grounds for unicorns), the better. With the cinnamon stick in your left hand and the apple in your right, stand comfortably and face east. Breathe and relax, feeling your feet anchored into the earth. Continue to relax and settle your mind until you see the first rays of the sun. As the sun just peeks above the horizon, place the apple on the ground next to the unicorn botanical and say:

> *Unicorn dwelling on this sacred land,*
> *I offer this gift to you straight from my hand.*
> *I am also here to request a boon:*
> *Please make me a magnet for cash, and soon!*
> *Your magic's more precious than credit or banks,*
> *So from deep in my heart, I offer you thanks.*

Hold the cinnamon stick in your open hands, cupped and facing out toward the rising sun. Feel the morning sunlight pouring into the cinnamon stick, enlivening it with magnetic and magical energy. Inwardly or aloud, give thanks once more to the unicorn that dwells on the land. Also thank the earth, the sky, and the rising sun. Keep the cinnamon stick with you until you receive the cash you need.

Spells for Romance and Friendship

Your true identity is love. This means it's natural for you to have a healthy love life and harmonious friendships. If you need support in these areas, these spells can help.

SPARKLE BATH TO ATTRACT A NEW ROMANCE

This sensational sparkle bath will attract a new romance into your life.

Ingredients

* * a sparkle bath bomb (available at Lush, Pacha Soap Co, and elsewhere)
* * a pink candle that has been rubbed with sunflower oil, rolled in pink glitter, and placed in a candle holder
* * your unicorn crystal
* * a lighter or matches

On a Friday when the moon is between new and full, light the candle in your bathroom and draw a warm bath by candlelight. When the bathtub is full, stand over it, hold your crystal in your right hand, and point it toward the water. Say:

> *Unicorn realm of sparkle and light,*
> *I ask your help with love this night.*
> *Very soon please help me meet*
> *A new love interest true and sweet.*

Feel sparkly light coming down from the highest sky, entering the crown of your head, moving down to your heart, down through your right arm, out of your crystal and into the water. When this feels complete, set the crystal near the bathtub, toss the sparkle bomb in the water, and get in after it. Soak for at least twenty minutes, feeling your body and energy field being drenched in the sparkly light of love. (This is not a time to wash, just to soak.)

When you get out of the bath, dry off and say:

> *Unicorns, thank you, thank you, thank you*
> *For all you are and all you do!*

Extinguish the candle and dress in something clean and lovely (pajamas or going-out clothes, according to your plans). Expect a new love interest to arrive in your life or be revealed from within your current circle of contacts within one moon cycle.

LILAC SPELL TO REPAIR A RELATIONSHIP

While not all relationships can or should be repaired (sometimes the best option is to walk away), there are some that are worth salvaging. If the relationship in question is the latter (whether friend, family, or love interest), this spell will help.

Ingredients
- a fresh lilac blossom (you can substitute a lavender blossom or a lavender rose blossom if lilac is not in season)
- aloe vera gel
- maple syrup
- a 4-ounce Mason jar with lid
- 2 tiny rectangles of paper, one with your name written on it and one with the other person's name written on it

Near your unicorn altar, or anywhere (indoors or out) where you won't be disturbed and that feels right for magic, sit comfortably in front of all the ingredients. Take some deep breaths and center your mind. When you feel relaxed and grounded, consciously connect with the unicorn realm. You can do this by calling your unicorn guides, picturing a unicorn or the unicorn realm in your mind, or conjuring up the feelings of bliss you get when you think about unicorns. When you feel tapped into your magic, put a tiny bit of aloe vera gel on your name and say:

May I now heal my heart.

Put a tiny bit of aloe vera gel on the other person's name and say:

May [name of person]'s heart now heal.

Place the rectangles of paper together so that the written names are touching each other. Say:

May our relationship now be repaired.

Put the rectangles of paper at the bottom of the jar and place the blossom on top. Say:

Blessings of beauty.

Pour maple syrup over the top of all of it and say:

Blessings of sweetness.

Close the lid and say:

Brought together in love, for the highest good of all.
Thank you, unicorns.
Thank you, Infinite Love.
Thank you, thank you, thank you.
Blessed be. And so it is.

Place the jar on your unicorn altar. Keep it there for one moon cycle, and then bury its contents at the base of a tree (ideally a unicorn-aligned tree—see chapter 7), using a spoon or small spatula to scoop it out. Rinse the jar, allow it to dry in bright sunlight, and feel free to reuse it in the future.

ANGEL AURA SPELL TO ATTRACT MAGICAL FRIENDSHIPS

We all need friends we love: people we can count on to laugh with us, comfort us when we cry, and help us out when we need a hand. Unicorn people like us also need at least one or two of those friends to share our magical, mysterious, wild, and wonderful worldview. This spell will help you attract friends who encompass all of the above.

Ingredient

* an angel aura quartz crystal point that has been cleansed in cool running water and bright sunlight (optionally, you can just use your unicorn crystal)

With the crystal in your left hand, sit comfortably in front of your unicorn altar. Relax and settle in as you take some long deep breaths. Then let your breathing be natural, but continue to notice as you breathe in and out. Continue being aware of your body and breathing until you feel very calm, clear, and centered.

Next, hold the crystal to your third eye as if it is a unicorn's horn. Imagine it is like an antennae broadcasting your signal as a unicorn devotee and initiate who is drawing upon your connection with the unicorns to summon others of like mind. Say:

> *Unicorns of the realm with which I'm aligned,*
> *Please send human allies of similar mind.*
> *Let us sparkle and dance and play in the sun,*
> *And spin spells in moonlight for love and for fun.*
> *Please send out my signal so it's loud and clear,*
> *Please send out my signal to those who would hear.*
> *I thank you, dear unicorns, for answering my call,*
> *Thank you, oh thank you, to one and to all.*

Place the crystal on your altar, and leave it there until your spell has had its desired effect.

Spells for Health and Healing

Heal yourself on the magical level and all other forms of healing will follow. These spells will help you establish holistic wellness inside and out.

RED CLOVER POTION FOR HEALING THE HEART

If your heart is aching or broken, you feel uncomfortably sensitive to the painful emotions of others, or you're healing from any sort of emotional pain, this potion can help.

Ingredients

* 1–3 teaspoons dried red clover blossoms placed in a white bowl and empowered in bright sunlight
* a tea strainer, tea ball, or muslin tea bag
* a mug
* a kettle
* water

Using the strainer, tea ball, or muslin bag, brew a cup of clover blossom tea. Allow it to steep for 10–15 minutes, strain or remove tea ball or tea bag, then drink. As you drink, feel your heart light becoming stronger, brighter, and healthier. Feel yourself being fortified with courage and infused with love. Repeat daily for as long as your heart could use some extra support.

CEDAR SPELL TO SPEED PHYSICAL HEALING

This simple practice will help speed physical healing for yourself or someone else.

Ingredients

* cedar essential oil
* an essential oil diffuser

Sit in front of your unicorn altar. Relax, breathe deeply, and center yourself. When you feel ready, hold the bottle of cedar essential oil in both hands. Consciously draw upon your connection to the unicorn realm. Tap into the pure strengthening and healing vibrations that are in the unicorn's magical repertoire and consciously channel them into the bottle. See and sense the bottle becoming filled with golden-white light like the sun. Feel gratitude and inwardly thank the unicorns for sharing their magical healing power. Place the diffuser in the same room with the healing person and diffuse the cedar. Diffuse for at least an hour each day while the patient is near, refreshing the oil regularly, for as long as is needed.

APPLE RITUAL FOR BOOSTING HEALTH AND IMMUNITY

This ritual will help bring back your natural state of vibrant health and powerful immunity.

Ingredients
* 5 clean organic apples on a white plate

On a Sunday when the moon is between new and full, place the plate of apples in bright sunlight for a minute or two. Imagine them soaking in the bright, bolstering light and becoming vibrant, glowing powerhouses of magical healing energy.

Next, call on your solar unicorn guide. While holding an image of this guide in your mind's eye, eat an apple and feel yourself internalizing the powerful light of the sun. Tomorrow repeat with another apple. Continue daily (for five days total) until you've eaten every apple.

Spells for Luck and Success

Do you feel lucky? If not, these spells have got you covered. The time is right to step into an expansive field of endless success.

CENTAURY COURAGE POTION

Before luck or success can manifest, we must have the courage to put ourselves out there and give ourselves a chance. This potion is simple, but it's just the thing for super-sensitive unicorn people who are tired of hiding in the shadows and are ready to step out into the sun.

Ingredients

* centaury flower essence (available online and at many health food stores as a Bach Flower Remedy)
* your reusable water bottle

Please note that a flower essence is a gentle homeopathic remedy that is taken internally. This is something entirely different than an essential oil, which contains highly concentrated plant material and should not be taken internally.

Twice a day for thirty days, turn your everyday drinking water into a potion by adding two drops of centaury flower essence directly from the dropper that comes in the bottle. Then, hold your drinking water bottle in both hands, call on your solar and unicorn guides and ask them to infuse your water with an extra dose of courage. Feel/ sense/imagine yourself feeling joyful as you speak out boldly, try the things you want to try, and do the things you want to do. (This can take less than a minute.) Drink the water throughout the day as you usually would.

MINT LUCK-WELCOMING RITUAL

This ritual employs the fresh magic of mint to invite luck into your home and life.

Ingredients
* ✷ 2 mint plants in pots (choose any variety that will thrive in your area)
* ✷ 2 clear quartz crystals

Just before or during sunrise on the day of a new moon, place the potted mint plants in your front yard, somewhere where you will walk through them to get to your front door. They could be on either side of the front door itself, on either side of your doorstep, or anywhere along the walk. Stand between them and face away from your house. Call in the unicorns by saying (or whispering or even saying to yourself silently) something like this:

> *Unicorns, I call you! Please send your magic*
> *to these mint plants. May they be lucky, and*
> *may they fill my life with luck. Thank you!*

Every time you water your mint, feel you are feeding the magic. And when you walk between the pots, feel you are being blessed and enlivened with lucky energy. Remember that herbs like to be picked, so as your mint grows and thrives, be sure to harvest some of it now and then so it will continue to thrive. (Of course, anything you add it to will have an extra dose of luck.)

When the growing season has ended and your mint ceases to thrive, harvest what you can and uproot the rest. Add it back to the earth or to a compost bin. Replace each pot with one of the clear quartz crystals to retain the lucky energy and hold the space for next year. Then, when the time is right in your area, replace the plants with two fresh ones and repeat the ritual once more.

MOONSTONE SUCCESS CHARM

Sunlight and sunny energy are usually used for success charms, but this one comes at it from a subtler (but no less powerful) angle, perfect for many of us sensitive unicorn types. You might want to weave this bit of magic before an endeavor you care about, such as a job interview, a test, a presentation, etc.

Ingredient
* a piece of moonstone jewelry you will like to wear

On the night of a full moon, when the moon is bright, find somewhere safe outside where you will be undisturbed. Hold the moonstone jewelry in your open right palm so it can soak in the moonlight. Summon your lunar unicorn guide by lovingly speaking its name. When you feel your guide's presence in the moonlight, say:

> *Thank you for being here, guide of the moon.*
> *Thank you for granting this magical boon.*
> *This luminous moonstone I ask you to bless,*
> *So I may be bathed in the light of success.*

Feel and sense your charm being infused with the magical energy you've summoned. Take another moment to feel even more gratitude for your unicorn guide's blessing, then hold the charm to your heart. Wear it when you want to ensure your success.

For more than one endeavor, refresh the magic by repeating the spell on a subsequent full moon.

Every person who fulfills his or her highest personal destiny creates a shift of healing for all living things.

Collette Baron-Reid in
THE WISDOM OF THE HIDDEN
REALMS GUIDEBOOK

UNICORN PORTAL KEY #11:

Lift the Veil

For this final portal exercise, find or create a cloth to serve as a veil. This could be a beautiful scarf, tablecloth, or light tapestry. Make sure it is made of a breathable 100 percent plant-based fabric such as cotton, linen, or bamboo. Ideal colors include white, vanilla, lilac, and sky blue. You will also need a single clear quartz crystal.

On the day of a new moon (or up to five days immediately following the new moon), go outside on a sunny day. On a table, lawn, or other outdoor surface, spread the cloth out in the sunshine. Set the crystal in the sunshine too. Let them bathe in the light for about two minutes or so, then flip the cloth over so the other side can soak in the sun for another couple of minutes.

Next, fold up the cloth, pocket the crystal, and go somewhere beautiful in nature where you won't be disturbed. (This could be the same location or a different one.) A forest, meadow, lake, pond, stream, or waterfall—i.e., unicorn stomping grounds—would all be great options if you have something like that nearby.

Sit comfortably in the natural location and breathe deeply. Relax, settle your mind, and come into the moment. Listen to the sounds around you and feel the fresh air on your skin. Simply enjoy being present, knowing that nature is all around you and that you are a part of nature too.

When you feel ready, cover your head and shoulders with the cloth veil. While it covers your face, summon both of your unicorn guides by lovingly speaking their names. Then, from your heart, speak words of commitment to your unicorn-aligned spiritual path. For example, you might say something like:

I vow to live a life of wonder. I vow to be a devotee
of love. I shall believe in magic, and I shall tread
lightly and gratefully in the realm of the unicorns,
with respect, admiration, and immense love.
I promise to be an ally to the unicorns and to walk
this path with courage and pride. Unicorns, I thank
you for welcoming me to your realm and for filling
my life with beauty and power. Thank you.

Know that as you lift the veil (provided you have completed all the other key exercises up to this point and provided you continue to walk the path with integrity), you will be wholly initiated into the realm. Its majestic power will be fully opened to you, and you can access it throughout your life to heal and create positive change.

Look around the world with fresh eyes. Know that you have been welcomed into the realm, and feel grateful. Express gratitude to your unicorn guides and allies.

The veil is your key. You can now wear it as a vestment of power (like a neck or head scarf) when you perform your unicorn devotions, meditations, and rituals. When it's not in use, fold it up and place the quartz on top of it to preserve its sacred power. Every couple months or so, recharge the veil and the crystal in bright sunlight as you did before.

CONCLUSION

At this time on earth, we need powerful priests and priest-esses to heal what is broken and to courageously magnify the values of wonder, purity, devotion, and love. You are one of these. On behalf of the unicorns, the cosmos, and the entire natural world, thank you for heeding the call, making the journey, and stepping into your place as one of these sacred keepers of the light. Great waves of positive vibrations are now emanating from your unique point of power on this great and magical earth. The transformational effects of this cannot be overstated.

Remember: you are powerful, you are beautiful, and you are never alone. The earth is alive, all living beings are your family, and the whole world is your home.

BIBLIOGRAPHY

Alexander, Skye. *Unicorns: The Myths, Legends, and Lore.* Avon, MA: Adams Media, 2015.

Andrews, Ted. *Treasures of the Unicorn: The Return to the Sacred Quest.* Batavia, OH: Dragonhawk Publishing, 1996.

Bradley, Josephine. *In Pursuit of the Unicorn.* Corte Madera, CA: Pomegranate Artbooks, 1980.

Calista. *Unicorn Rising: Live Your Truth and Unleash Your Magic.* Carlsbad, CA: Hay House, 2018.

Cooper, Diana. *The Wonder of Unicorns.* Findhorn, Forres, Scotland: Findhorn Press, 2008.

Cunningham, Scott. *Cunningham's Encyclopedia of Magical Herbs.* St. Paul, MN: Llewellyn, 1985.

Einstein, Albert. *Bite-Size Einstein: Quotations on Just About Everything from the Greatest Mind of the Twentieth Century.* Compiled by Jerry Mayer and John P. Holms. New York: Random House, 1996.

Gray, Joanna. *Be More Unicorn: How to Find Your Inner Sparkle.* London: Quadrille, 2018.

Hathaway, Nancy. *The Unicorn*. New York: Penguin, 1982.

Judith, Anodea. *Chakras: Seven Keys to Awakening and Healing the Energy Body*. Carlsbad, CA: Hay House, 2016.

Kondo, Marie. *The Life-Changing Magic of Tidying Up: The Japanese Art of Decluttering and Organizing*. Berkeley: Ten Speed Press, 2014.

Lembo, Margaret Ann. *The Essential Guide to Crystals, Minerals, and Stones*. Woodbury, MN: Llewellyn, 2013.

Medici, Marina. *Good Magic*. New York: Simon & Schuster, 1988.

Melody. *Love Is in the Earth: A Kaleidoscope of Crystals*. Wheat Ridge, CO: Earth-Love Publishing House, 1995.

Perls, Fredrick S. *Gestalt Therapy Verbatim*. Compiled and edited by John O. Stevens. Lafayette, CA: Real People Press, 1969.

Roosevelt, Eleanor. *The Autobiography of Eleanor Roosevelt*. New York: Harper Collins, 1937.

Scheffer, Mechthild. *The Encyclopedia of Bach Flower Therapy*. Rochester, VT: Healing Arts Press, 2001.

Simons, Adela. *A Unicorn in Your Living-Room: A Guide to Spiritual Illumination*. Leicestershire, UK: Matador, 2014.

Venefica, Avia. www.whats-your-sign.com.

————. www.symbolic-meanings.com.

Whitehurst, Tess. *The Magic of Flowers: A Guide to Their Metaphysical Uses & Properties*. Woodbury, MN: Llewellyn, 2013.

————. *The Magic of Trees: A Guide to Their Sacred Wisdom & Metaphysical Properties*. Woodbury, MN: Llewellyn, 2017.